Learning Einstein Analytics

Unlock critical insights with Salesforce Einstein Analytics

Santosh Tukaram Chitalkar

BIRMINGHAM - MUMBAI

Learning Einstein Analytics

Commissioning Editor: Richa Tripathi
Acquisition Editor: Karan Sadawana
Content Development Editor: Zeeyan Pinheiro
Technical Editor: Vibhuti Gawde
Copy Editor: Safis Editing
Project Coordinator: Vaidehi Sawant
Proofreader: Safis Editing
Indexer: Francy Puthiry
Graphics: Jason Monteiro
Production Coordinator: Arvindkumar Gupta

First published: January 2018

Production reference: 1250118

Published by Packt Publishing Ltd.
Livery Place
35 Livery Street
Birmingham
B3 2PB, UK.

ISBN 978-1-78847-576-1

www.packtpub.com

This is my first book and I want to dedicate my humble efforts to my family. Mom, Dad, and my wife Anuradha, who have never complained about my workaholic nature. I could write this book only because of their love and support. A special thanks to my mentor Rohit Arora, who believed in me, pushed me, and helped me find my passion for technology. Only he believed in my ability and to achieve success to this extent. I feel blessed to have such special people around me.

`mapt.io`

Mapt is an online digital library that gives you full access to over 5,000 books and videos, as well as industry leading tools to help you plan your personal development and advance your career. For more information, please visit our website.

Why subscribe?

- Spend less time learning and more time coding with practical eBooks and Videos from over 4,000 industry professionals

- Improve your learning with Skill Plans built especially for you

- Get a free eBook or video every month

- Mapt is fully searchable

- Copy and paste, print, and bookmark content

PacktPub.com

Did you know that Packt offers eBook versions of every book published, with PDF and ePub files available? You can upgrade to the eBook version at `www.PacktPub.com` and as a print book customer, you are entitled to a discount on the eBook copy. Get in touch with us at `service@packtpub.com` for more details.

At `www.PacktPub.com`, you can also read a collection of free technical articles, sign up for a range of free newsletters, and receive exclusive discounts and offers on Packt books and eBooks.

Contributors

About the author

Santosh Tukaram Chitalkar has been working on the Salesforce platform for over five years. He currently works for Capgemini as a Salesforce consultant. During his time at Capgemini, he has worked on various Salesforce projects, which include the implementation of sales SFO, inline Visualforce pages for sales and service assets, and renewal processes.

He has also developed products for AppExchange such as FieldRecon. In his free time, he loves writing about Salesforce Einstein Analytics on his blog Pinakin Technology.

About the reviewer

Abhishek Tripathi has more than 5 years of experience with the Salesforce platform. He is a Salesforce certified application architect and has 16 Salesforce certifications. He is a technical blogger, posting tips and tricks for Salesforce to help others in the Salesforce community.

Abhishek has worked with some giants with Salesforce, such as PwC US, Coca-Cola, Tquila (acquired by Accenture), and Accenture.

Packt is searching for authors like you

If you're interested in becoming an author for Packt, please visit authors.packtpub.com and apply today. We have worked with thousands of developers and tech professionals, just like you, to help them share their insight with the global tech community. You can make a general application, apply for a specific hot topic that we are recruiting an author for, or submit your own idea.

Table of Contents

Preface

Einstein Analytics, formally known as Wave Analytics, is a cloud-based platform that connects data from multiple sources and explores it to uncover insights. It empowers sales representatives, marketers, and analysts with insights to make customer interactions smarter; without building mathematical models. You will learn how to create applications, lenses, and dashboards, and how to share those dashboards with other users.

This book starts off by explaining the fundamental concepts, such as lenses, steps, and measures; it then sets you up with the Einstein Analytics platform. The book then moves on to creating an application—you will learn how to create datasets and dashboards, and the different ways of importing data into Analytics. Moving on, we look at Einstein for sales, services, and marketing, individually. Here, you will learn to manage your pipeline, understand important business drivers, and visualize trends. You will also learn features related to data monitoring tools and embedding dashboards with Lightning, Visualforce page, and mobile devices. Further, you will learn advanced features pertaining to the recent advancements in Einstein, which include machine learning constructs and getting predictions for events. By the end of this book, you will be proficient in Einstein Analytics, getting insights faster and understanding your customers in a better way.

Who this book is for

This book is for beginners who want to explore this AI-powered business intelligence software by Salesforce. Prior knowledge of the Salesforce platform is required.

What this book covers

Chapter 1, *Getting Started with Einstein Analytics*, gives an overview of Einstein Analytics. It also covers the concepts and terminologies used in Einstein Analytics. We will sign up to Salesforce special developer edition in this chapter.

Chapter 2, *Setting Up Einstein Analytics*, covers creating and understanding users and user types. We are going to learn how to create and assign permission sets.

Chapter 3, *Say Hello to Einstein*, covers building your first lenses and dashboards.

Chapter 4, *Diving Deep into Einstein Analytics*, covers creating a simple summary dashboard and understanding quota, dataflow, and dataflow scheduling. This chapter also explains Classic Designer Dashboard and Wave Designer Dashboard. In addition, it will cover faceting and declarative binding.

Chapter 5, *Einstein for Sales*, explains how to create an executive dashboard. While creating dashboards, you will learn about creating static steps, selection, and result binding.

Chapter 6, *Einstein at Your Service*, covers creating a service dashboard. While creating a dashboard, you will learn about the dashboard inspector and connecting your static step with dashboard components.

Chapter 7, *Security and Sharing in Einstein Analytics*, is an important chapter as it covers security and sharing in Einstein Analytics. This chapter covers Salesforce data access, data sharing, and data security, while also taking you through adding row-level security to a dataset.

Chapter 8, *Recipe in Einstein*, covers how to create a recipe. When working with data, there are times when we realize that we have added a lot of unnecessary fields and data, and we need to remove them. We also need to add new fields to the same dataset if we have missed a required field or, if we need to add a new one in the future. This is called data preparation and it is easier with Einstein Analytics.

Chapter 9, *Embedding Einstein Dashboards*, is all about Einstein Analytics providing the flexibility to embed dashboards within other Salesforce environments. It covers all the different methods of embedding dashboards and adding filters to embedded dashboards.

Chapter 10, *Advanced Technologies in Einstein Analytics*, covers advanced technologies or methods in Einstein Analytics. This chapter also covers the use of JSON, XMD, and SAQL for working on complex solutions.

Chapter 11, *Machine Learning and Deep Learning*, gives an overview of machine learning, deep learning, and NLP. You will also see the implementation of all these technologies in Einstein Analytics: Einstein Language and Einstein Sentiment.

To get the most out of this book

Learning Einstein Analytics is for all Salesforce CRM techies who wish to learn this platform. We have written this book keeping beginners in mind, but it is important that you are familiar with Salesforce CRM. Basic concepts and admin knowledge of Salesforce is required.

Einstein Analytics is a cloud-based platform; hence, you only need a system with a good internet connection to get started with this book. The first two chapters of this book explain the basic concepts and terminologies of Einstein Analytics and its setup. In Chapter 3, *Say Hello to Einstein*, Chapter 4, *Diving deep into Einstein Analytics*, Chapter 5, *Einstein for Sales*, and Chapter 6, *Einstein at Your Service*, the book explains the platform in detail and uses hands-on tutorials to explain how it works. We have taken a few business requirements from a hypothetical organization called Anutosh Infotech and we'll be building sales and service dashboards for that organization. While creating these dashboards, we will go through every relevant concept, feature, and implementation. The last five chapters explain how to build a complex solution in Einstein Analytics and give an overview of the advanced technologies and features provided by the Einstein platform.

Download the example code files

You can download the example code files for this book from your account at www.packtpub.com. If you purchased this book elsewhere, you can visit www.packtpub.com/support and register to have the files emailed directly to you.

You can download the code files by following these steps:

1. Log in or register at www.packtpub.com.
2. Select the **SUPPORT** tab.
3. Click on **Code Downloads & Errata**.
4. Enter the name of the book in the **Search** box and follow the onscreen instructions.

Once the file is downloaded, please make sure that you unzip or extract the folder using the latest version of:

- WinRAR/7-Zip for Windows
- Zipeg/iZip/UnRarX for Mac
- 7-Zip/PeaZip for Linux

The code bundle for the book is also hosted on GitHub at `https://github.com/PacktPublishing/Learning-Einstein-Analytics`. We also have other code bundles from our rich catalog of books and videos available at `https://github.com/PacktPublishing/`. Check them out!

Download the color images

We also provide a PDF file that has color images of the screenshots/diagrams used in this book. You can download it here: `http://www.packtpub.com/sites/default/files/downloads/LearningEinsteinAnalytics_ColorImages.pdf`.

Conventions used

There are a number of text conventions used throughout this book.

`CodeInText`: Indicates code words in text, database table names, folder names, filenames, file extensions, pathnames, dummy URLs, user input, and Twitter handles. Here is an example: "Create a report on an account, export it to a CSV file named `Account_data.csv`, and save it to your local drive."

A block of code is set as follows:

```
[ "Account.BillingCountry",
        "{{column(Static_Country_1.selection, [\"value\"]).asObject()}}",
        "in"
        ],
```

When we wish to draw your attention to a particular part of a code block, the relevant lines or items are set in bold:

```
[default]
exten => s,1,Dial(Zap/1|30)
exten => s,2,Voicemail(u100)
exten => s,102,Voicemail(b100)
exten => i,1,Voicemail(s0)
```

Bold: Indicates a new term, an important word, or words that you see onscreen. For example, words in menus or dialog boxes appear in the text like this. Here is an example: "Click on **Enable Analytics**, as shown in the following screenshot."

Warnings or important notes appear like this.

 Tips and tricks appear like this.

Get in touch

Feedback from our readers is always welcome.

General feedback: Email `feedback@packtpub.com` and mention the book title in the subject of your message. If you have questions about any aspect of this book, please email us at `questions@packtpub.com`.

Errata: Although we have taken every care to ensure the accuracy of our content, mistakes do happen. If you have found a mistake in this book, we would be grateful if you would report this to us. Please visit `www.packtpub.com/submit-errata`, selecting your book, clicking on the Errata Submission Form link, and entering the details.

Piracy: If you come across any illegal copies of our works in any form on the Internet, we would be grateful if you would provide us with the location address or website name. Please contact us at `copyright@packtpub.com` with a link to the material.

If you are interested in becoming an author: If there is a topic that you have expertise in and you are interested in either writing or contributing to a book, please visit `authors.packtpub.com`.

Reviews

Please leave a review. Once you have read and used this book, why not leave a review on the site that you purchased it from? Potential readers can then see and use your unbiased opinion to make purchase decisions, we at Packt can understand what you think about our products, and our authors can see your feedback on their book. Thank you!

For more information about Packt, please visit `packtpub.com`.

1
Getting Started with Einstein Analytics

The evolution of technology has increased to a new level in the last five years and **Customer Relationship Management** (**CRM**) is an integral part of it. CRM has helped companies manage and analyze customer interactions and data throughout the customer life cycle, with the goal of improving business relationships with customers. But the analysis of data, managing it, and making business decisions based on that customer data is becoming more and more challenging because of the social media, internet, and technology. With a huge amount of customer data growing exponentially, extracting patterns, business trends, and actionable information is becoming a tedious and time-consuming task for organizations worldwide. Data generation, processing, and consumption are simple but converting that data to spot opportunities, trends, and correlation is a real challenge. In order to effectively tackle this situation, Salesforce has launched its most advanced platform called **Einstein Analytics**.

Pretty catchy name, right?

The Einstein Analytics platform has really become a buzz word in the tech town. So what is this Einstein Analytics? Why is there such a buzz about it? Why is everybody talking about it since its launch?

In this chapter, we will cover the following topics:

- The Einstein Analytics platform
- An introduction to Einstein Analytics

Einstein Analytics

Einstein Analytics is a comprehensive business intelligence tool powered by artificial intelligence, and used to analyze all your business data in quick succession for precise predictive insights and prescriptive recommendations.

Introduction to Einstein Analytics

Salesforce users will get recommendations and suggestions automatically. The Einstein Analytics platform learns from the customer data already in Salesforce and makes predictions accordingly. Insights, predictions, and recommendations are served up seamlessly in Salesforce.

Consider this scenario, Anutosh Infotech is a multinational organization that launched a new product called **All Smart**. All Smart is a tracking device that connects your belongings to the All Smart application on your phone and helps you find them. Now, to create awareness of this product, Anutosh Infotech started publicizing it via ads on Facebook, YouTube, and so on and they got the xyz number of leads through it. Now Einstein will automatically give a recommendation about which campaign is more effective. So for the next campaign, the company will spend more money on effective campaigning. You can also share multiple insights regarding this campaign's **Lead Scoring**, **Einstein Recommendations**, **Einstein Social Insights**, and so on.

The Salesforce document clearly states the following:

> *"Einstein is like having your own data scientist to guide you through your day. It learns from all your data, and delivers predictions and recommendations based on your unique business processes."*

In Einstein Analytics, we can gather data from different locations, such as Excel, Salesforce, Informatica, and so on and merge them together to build the insights.

Here are the main reasons why Einstein is the next big thing:

- Social media is a platform where customers give their feedback about products and services. So the data on social media will play an important role and this data is increasing exponentially each day.
- Einstein Analytics uses new technologies such as advanced machine learning, deeper understanding, predictive analytics, natural language processing, and smart data discovery. So, with every interaction and every additional piece of data, it will learn and self-tune to get smarter.
- Einstein Analytics uses predictive analysis and gives recommendations based on the data history.
- User can connect to data on other platforms and built dashboards on it. The user can also import that data to Einstein Analytics without any formulas or coding.
- Einstein is secure, trusted, scalable, dependable, and, of course, mobile! It enables everyone in your organization to get instant access to powerful statistics and figures through its intuitive point and click visual interface.
- It promises to help sales, marketing, and service professionals make better decisions, up to 38% faster by leveraging artificial intelligence. It proposes to achieve this via contextually relevant, self-service Analytics applications that can tell you what is happening, why it is happening, what is likely to happen, and what action you should take.

From the sales, marketing, or services standpoint, this smart, artificially intelligent tool is helping businesses understand the results of their different activities better.

You may ask, what is so great about Einstein Analytics or how it is different from the already present Analytics tool.

The answer to these questions is simple. Einstein Analytics allows users to note performance data to get an insight into different activities and their results. This is quite like the other tools, but here is how it is different:

- Its artificial intelligence analyzes productivity and automatically gives insights and recommendations for informed decision making
- It includes the following entire pool of Analytics applications to expose more in-depth and futuristic information:
  - Service Analytics
  - Sales Analytics
  - B2B Marketing Analytics

With Einstein Analytics, every CRM user can now easily analyze what happened in the business, why it happened, and what steps to take, without a team of expert data scientists.

Salesforce is partnering with **Trailhead**, an interactive, guided, and gamified learning platform that offers 12 online learning modules. Trounce your competitors and get a head start by learning Einstein Analytics with Trailhead.

To start learning, go through the following tutorials:

- Analytics/Wave Basics
- Mobile Analytics / Wave Exploration
- Desktop Analytics / Wave Exploration

If you are working with Salesforce as a partner, the following are specific training programs for you:

- White belt
- Green belt
- Brown belt
- Black belt

Terminologies in Einstein Analytics

Einstein Analytics is a cloud-based data platform as well as a data-analysis frontend, and it's designed to analyze not just Salesforce sales, service, and marketing data, but also any third-party application data, desktop data, or public data you care to bring into the mix.

So, sign up for Salesforce Einstein Analytics and get started by visiting `https://developer.salesforce.com/promotions/orgs/analytics-de`. The link will take you to a site that resembles this:

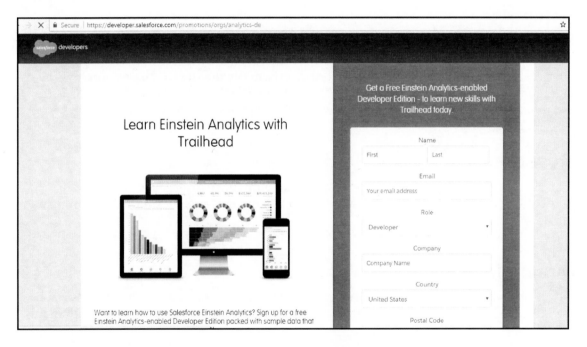

Now that you have signed up for the special developer edition, let me walk you through the basic concepts and terminologies used in Einstein Analytics.

Concepts - terminologies

Before starting with Einstein Analytics, we need to understand the basic concepts and terminologies. This section will help you to understand, how the Einstein Analytics platform works and the significance of different terminologies. Understanding this concept is very important as it avoids confusion during the implementation and hands-on tutorials.

So without further ado, let's begin our journey of learning Einstein Analytics.

Datasets

A dataset is a collection of related data that is stored in a denormalized, yet highly compressed form. You can create the dataset from different resources such as Excel, Salesforce, or other databases. In other words, you can say that it is a data resource, specially formatted to create analytics and reports on it. In Einstein Analytics, all the fields of dataset come under three categories such as date, dimension, and measure.

Measures

A measure is a quantitative value, for example, amount, price, profit, and loss. Measure can be used to make mathematical calculations such as sum, average, maximum, minimum, and so on.

Dimensions

A dimension is a qualitative value, for example, city, region, and status. Dimensions can be used to create grouping and filtering. As it is a qualitative value, you cannot do math in this field.

Dates

A date can be represented as a day, month, year, and, optionally, time. We can use the date field to group, filter, and perform math.

Dataset builder

Dataset builder is a point and click UI feature provided by Salesforce to create datasets. You can create a single dataset for a Salesforce object. Data can be created based on one or more related Salesforce objects.

Lenses

A lens is a particular view of a dataset's data. Just like reports in Salesforce, the lens provides insights into data. This helps you analyze and visualize your data.

Visualizations

 A visualization is a pictorial representation of dashboards, application, and lenses. Commonly, it can be a line chart, bar chart, stack chart, tables, pivots, or compare tables. Every visualization has a query associated with it.

Dashboards

A dashboard is a collection of charts, metrics, and tables. We can have one or more lenses in one dashboard.

Designers

A designer is a user interface where a user can create dashboards.

Dashboard JSON

Dashboard JSON is the JSON file for your dashboard. This file includes the information related to your widgets, their location, settings, static steps, and how they are connected.

Explorer

An explorer is an interface where you explore datasets and lenses. It is the easiest way to access your business data and get data insights. Using the explorer, users can add measures, grouping, filters, and so on. In the UI, users can switch between **Chart Mode**, **Table Mode**, and **SAQL Mode**.

Apps

An application is a curated set of one or more dashboards and lenses. For example, If you have created four dashboards for the sales team and two dashboards for the service team then you can create two separate applications (like the folder) one for the sales team and another for the service team and move the dashboards and lenses to the respective applications.

Transformation

A transformation refers to the manipulation of data. You can add transformations to a dataflow to extract data from Salesforce objects or datasets, transform datasets that contain Salesforce or external data, and register datasets.

For example, you can use transformations to join data from two related datasets and then register the resulting dataset to make it available for queries.

SAQL

Salesforce Analytics Query Language (SAQL) is used to access data from a dataset. It is a query language for Analytics platform. Just like all other query languages, SAQL retrieves data from the dataset. Lenses and dashboards also use SAQL behind the scenes. It gathers the meaningful data for visualizations. We can use SAQL to handle complex views such as working with multiple datasets to get a single view.

Predicate

A predicate is a filter condition that defines row-level access for each record from the dataset. Define a predicate for each dataset on which you want to restrict access to records. In other words, row-level security is enforced by the predicate.

Metadata files

A metadata file is a JSON file that describes the structure of an external data file.

Dataflow

You can use a dataflow to create one or more datasets based on data from Salesforce objects or existing datasets. A dataflow is a set of instructions that specify what data to extract from Salesforce objects or datasets, how to transform the datasets, and which datasets to make available for querying.

Dataflow jobs

A dataflow job processes the logic in a dataflow.

For example, after creating a dataset, it will create a process that will kick-start the dataset creation process. We can monitor dataflow jobs from the data manager.

Summary

In this chapter, you learned that Einstein Analytics is a cloud-based platform for connecting data from multiple sources, creating interactive views of that data, and sharing those views in applications. We saw that it is a better way to distribute insights to business users so that they can understand and take action on changing information. It is also powered by artificial intelligence, which means that you have your own data scientist. For a quick start and a fun way to start with Einstein Analytics, we went through Trailhead tutorials or badges. The regular developer organization does not have Einstein Analytics, so you signed up for a special developer edition at `https://developer.Salesforce.com/promotions/orgs/analytics-de`, where you have a specific training program if you are working with Salesforce as a partner. Also, we covered the concepts and terminologies of Einstein Analytics.

In next chapter, we will cover the Einstein Analytics setup. We will also see how to create permissions. We will explore user types and user licenses here. Einstein Analytics also has limitations and these will be covered in the next chapter.

2
Setting Up Einstein Analytics

Before starting to build the dashboard, lenses, and applications, it is important to set your organization and define user types so that they are available to use. We discussed concepts and terminologies and the importance of Einstein Analytics in the previous chapter. This chapter walks you through simple steps that will set up your organization to use the Einstein Analytics platform.

In this chapter, we will cover the following topics:

- The Einstein Analytics platform setup process
- Creating permission sets and user licenses
- Assigning permission set to users
- Einstein limits

The Einstein platform setup process

Now that you have logged in to your special developer edition for Einstein Analytics, let's set up your organization for Einstein. Following are the basic steps to set up Einstein Analytics:

1. Enable Einstein Analytics for your organization
2. Define the main Einstein user types
3. Create permission sets to group related user permissions according to the needs of each user type
4. Assign a permission set to an individual user, which also auto-assigns Analytics Cloud --the Einstein Analytics platform permission set license to that user

Enabling Analytics

Once you have signed up and verified your email ID, the next step is to log in to Salesforce. It is important to know that Salesforce provides two UI modes: Salesforce Classic and Lightning Experience. By default, Salesforce opens in Lightning Experience mode.

To switch to the Classic mode, click on the view profile icon in the top-right corner and click on **Switch to Salesforce Classic**:

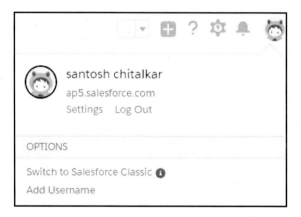

In order to use Einstein Analytics, first you need to enable it by performing the following steps:

1. Click on **Setup** in the top-right corner
2. Under **Administer**, navigate to **Analytics | Getting Started** as shown in the following screenshot:

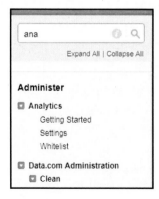

3. Click on **Enable Analytics**, as shown in the following screenshot:

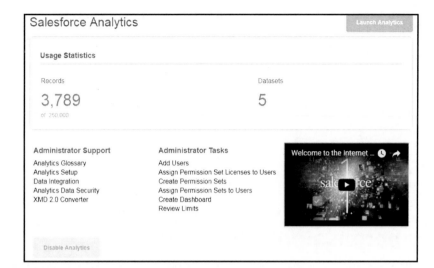

We have signed up for special developer edition, Analytics must be already enabled for you.

User types

Before creating permission sets, you need to know exactly what the user requirement is. Identifying and knowing user requirements helps you to create an efficient process that meets the requirements of your team.

There are the following two basic categories of user:

- **Users**: They only require to view data, insights, lenses, dashboards, and occasionally import data
- **Administrators or managers**: They require full access to Analytics to create datasets, lenses, visualizations, dashboards, and so on

Accordingly, you should create the following two basic permission sets:

- **View**: This permission set contains the permissions needed by most basic-level users when they access Analytics.

- **Manage**: This permission set has all rights. This permission set should be assigned to managers and system administrators who require complete access to Einstein Analytics. A user with manager permission can have access to all datasets and rights in Einstein Analytics.

You can define your own user types depending upon organization requirements as follows:

- A superuser having full access
- A data import master having data import permissions only
- A view-only user having view permissions only
- A moderate user having permissions for both data import and view

Here, we are creating only two permission sets.

Creating permission sets

Permission set licenses enable users to grant permissions to explore data and allow the user to manage it in Einstein. They also let Salesforce Community users view Einstein dashboards, as follows:

- All users who wants to access the Einstein Analytics platform should have the Analytics permission set.
- The community user must have the Einstein / Wave Community Users permission set license to view dashboards. Community users can see the applications shared via dashboards embedded in Visualforce pages.

The Analytics Cloud --Einstein Analytics platform permission set license enables the following permissions:

User permission	What it enables
Use Einstein Analytics	This enables accessing Einstein Analytics, viewing and exploring datasets, and viewing and sharing lenses and dashboards
Create and edit Einstein Analytics dashboards	This enables creating, editing, and deleting Einstein Analytics dashboards

To create permission sets, you will have to perform the following steps:

1. Go to the **Setup** menu.
2. Under **Administer**, navigate to **Manage Users | Permission Sets** and then click on **New**, as shown in the following screenshot:

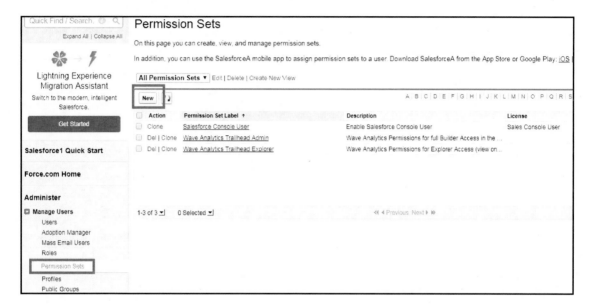

3. Give a label name under **Label** and an API name under **API Name**. Select the **License** type as **Analytics Cloud Integration User** and click on the **Save** button, as shown in the following screenshot:

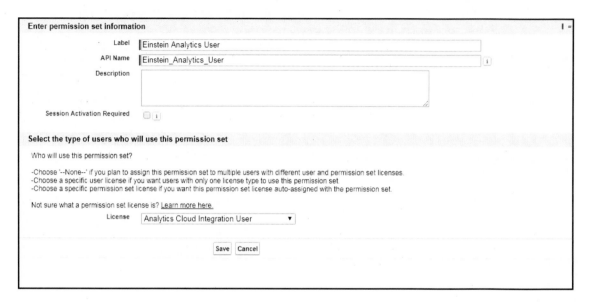

For efficiency, you can assign a permission set to groups of users. Also, you can assign multiple permission sets to a user.

Assigning a Einstein Analytics permission set to users

The next step in the setup process is to assign an Einstein Analytics permission set to users. When you assign a permission set license, any user assigned to the permission set is auto-assigned the permission set license. Perform the following simple steps to assign the permission set to the users:

1. Navigate to **Setup** | **Administer** | **Manage Users** | **Permission Sets**.

2. Select the permission which you created in the previous section.

3. Click on the **Manage Assignments** button:

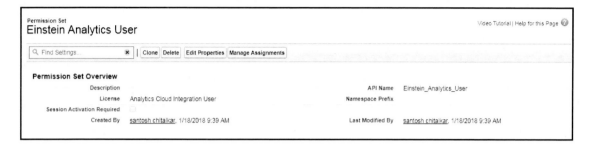

4. Now, click on the **Add Assignment** button:

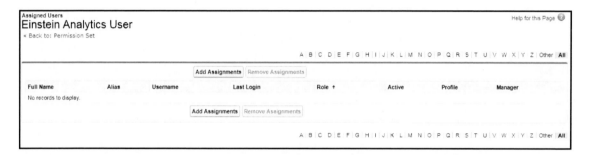

5. Select the user who needs access to Einstein Analytics by checking the checkbox. The user to whom you are assigning this permission must have license of type **Analytics Cloud Integration User**:

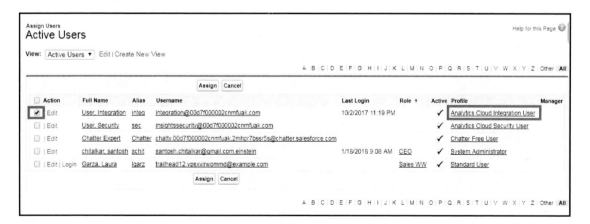

6. Click on the **Assign** button. Click on **Done** in the next screen, and the permission set will be assigned to the selected user:

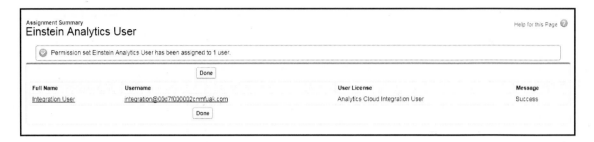

7. Now click on the **Settings** option under **Analytics**. Select the **Show preview thumbnails for secure lenses and dashboards** option.
8. Click on the **Save** button.

Enabling the **Show preview thumbnails for secure lenses and dashboards** option exposes sensitive data.

Now let's take a look at the following steps to learn how to control access to Salesforce objects and fields:

1. Navigate to **Setup** | **Administer** | **Manage Users** | **Profiles**. Select a user profile (for an integration user, select the **Analytics Cloud Integration User** profile, and for a security user, select the **Analytics Cloud Security User** profile):

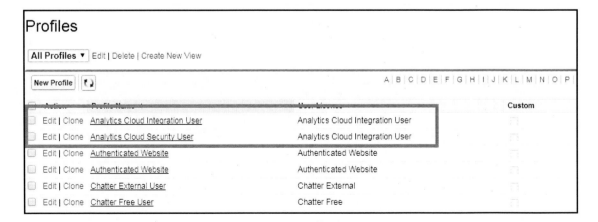

2. Click on **Clone**.

3. Provide the profile name and save the cloned user:

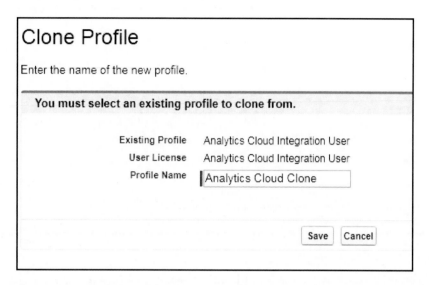

4. To enable permissions on the object, again follow the same path to profile which is **Setup** | **Administer** | **Manage Users** | **Profiles**.

5. Select the profile you just cloned.

6. Click on **Edit** and scroll down to the **Custom Object Permissions** section as shown in the following screenshot:

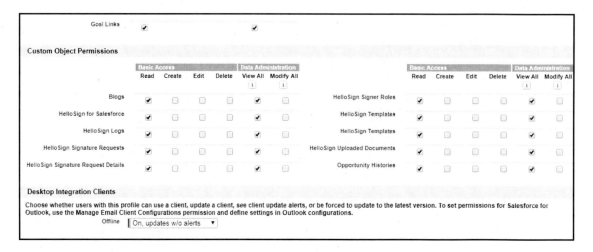

7. Select **Read** in the **Custom Object Permissions** section.
8. To enable a permission on a field of the object, select **Read** for the field in the **Field Permissions** section.
9. Click on **Save**.

Repeat these steps for each permission set. You assign the Wave platform permission set license when you create and assign this permission set to users in your organization.

Einstein limits

The Einstein Analytics platform license is a single-user license. There is a limit on how much data you can display on the table. Every Analytics platform license has limits on data storage, data display, features, and so on. But the data storage limits are contractual and not technical, so if we need to display more data than fits in the limit, then we need to purchase additional data rows.

Take a look at the following table:

License	Limit
Analytics Cloud --Wave Analytics Platform	100 million rows
Analytics Cloud --Sales Wave Analytics Application	25 million rows when used without Analytics Cloud --the Wave Analytics Platform license
Analytics Cloud --Service Wave Analytics Application	25 million rows when used without Analytics Cloud --the Wave Analytics Platform license
Analytics Cloud --Additional Data Rows	100 million rows

If you disable Einstein Analytics, user permissions are removed from each defined permission set automatically. If you re-enable Einstein Analytics later, you must define the permission sets again.

 Einstein Analytics license data storage limits are contractual, not technical. The license agrees to strictly monitor its total number of data rows.

Summary

You can build other permission sets out of individual permissions enabled by the Sales Analytics license, depending on the needs of users in your organization. In this chapter, you learned about the setup process of Analytics, and you also saw how to enable Analytics for your organization. We also covered how to create permission sets and define user types. The user types can change and increase depending on your requirement. Once you assign a permission set to a user, the permission set license is auto-assigned to that user.

In the next chapter, we will cover designing, creating, and scheduling dataflows.

We will also see what a dashboard is and the types of dashboard in Einstein Analytics. We will explore the use of pre-built dashboard templates and create a Wave Designer Dashboard using the **Summary Dashboard** template.

We will also see how to display data insights by using widgets.

3
Say Hello to Einstein

We have completed the setup process and built the permission sets. We know that user types can be created depending upon requirements and we can create a user type and assign the permissions accordingly. Once you assign a permission set to a user, the permission set license is auto-assigned to that user. Let's start with some hands-on tutorials. In the previous chapter, we assigned a permission set to users and gave access to Analytics. In this chapter, we will create our first dataset and dashboard. This chapter includes different methods of creating datasets. It also guides you through easy and simple steps to create lenses, dashboards, and applications.

In this chapter, we will cover the following topics:

- Data preparation
- Creating datasets
- Creating dashboards
- Creating lenses
- Visualizations
- Creating applications

Data preparation

In Einstein, all visualizations are built on datasets. A dataset is a collection of related data in the highly normalized form. You use data source in Einstein Analytics to create reports, dashboards, and business insights. We can create a dataset using the following three different methods:

- CSV
- Salesforce data
- Informatica Rev / external data source

The easiest way is to get a CSV file from reports. Let's take a look at the following steps:

1. Create a report on an account, export it to a CSV file named `Account_data.csv`, and save it to your local drive.
2. Let's go to Einstein Analytics. To open Einstein, open the **Trailhead Data Manager** drop-down list at the top-right corner and select **Analytics Studio**:

3. If you are in the Lightning mode, select **Analytics Studio** in the **App Launcher** section, as shown in the following screenshot:

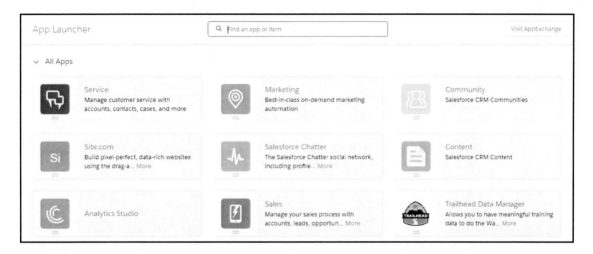

Hurrah!!!! You have successfully logged in to Einstein Analytics.

Let's get familiar with the environment and create your first dataset using the dataset builder:

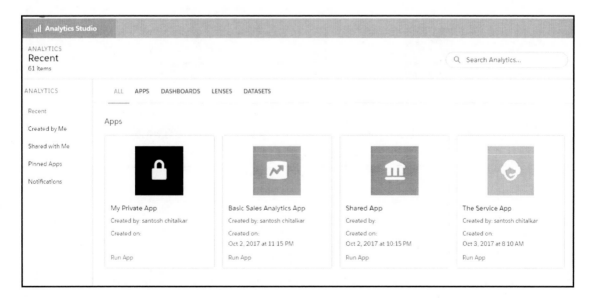

Analytics Studio is the area where you can see your Einstein platform applications; you can pin and unpin your applications to personalize your home page. If you click on the **ALL** tab, you can see all your applications, dashboards, lenses, and datasets on a single page.

Creating your first dataset

A dataset is a set of source data, specially formatted and optimized for interactive exploration. Here are the steps to create a new dataset:

1. Click on the **Create** button in the top-right corner and then click on **Dataset**. You can see the following three options to create datasets:
   - **CSV File**
   - **Salesforce**
   - **Informatica Rev**

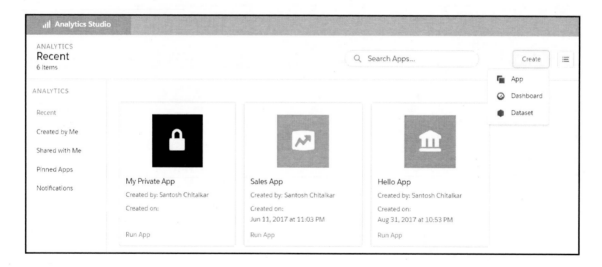

2. Select **CSV File** and click on **Continue**, as shown in the following screenshot:

3. Select the `Account_data.csv` file or drag and drop the file.

4. Click on **Next**. The next screen uploads the user interface to create a single dataset by using the `external.csv` file:

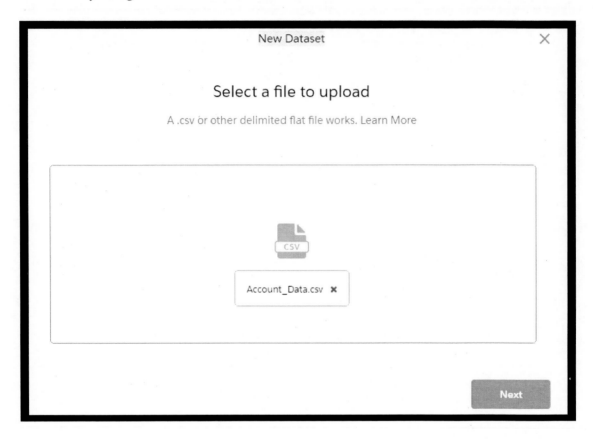

5. Click on **Next** to proceed as shown in the following screenshot:

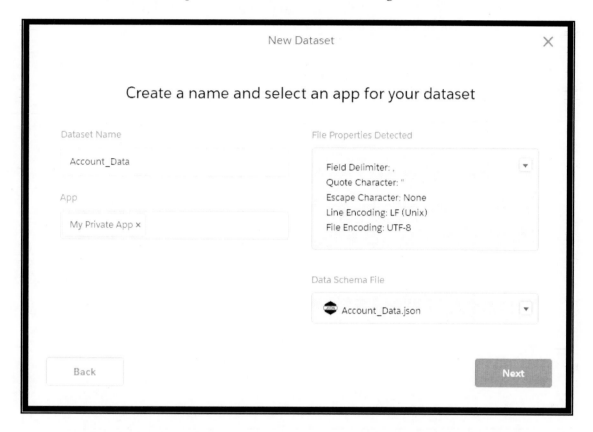

6. Change the dataset name if you want. You can select an application to store the dataset. You can also replace the CSV file from this screen.

7. Click on 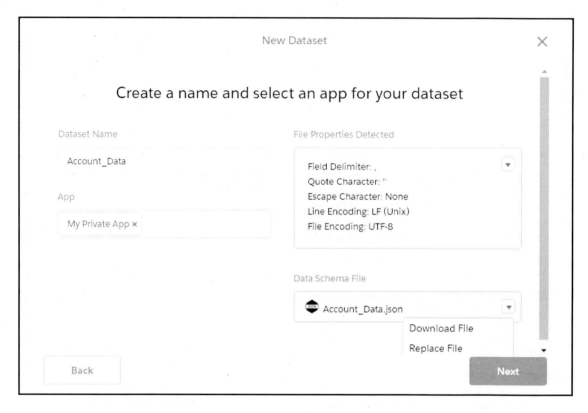 in the **Data Schema File** section and select the **Replace File** option to change the file. You can also download the uploaded .csv file from here as shown in the following screenshot:

New Dataset   ✕

Create a name and select an app for your dataset

Dataset Name   File Properties Detected

Account_Data   Field Delimiter: ,
                                                Quote Character: "
App   Escape Character: None
                                                Line Encoding: LF (Unix)
My Private App ×   File Encoding: UTF-8

                                                Data Schema File

                                                📄 Account_Data.json   ▾
                                                            Download File
                                                            Replace File

Back   Next

8. Click on **Next**. In the next screen, you can change field attributes such as column name, dimensions, field type, and so on.
9. Click on the **Next** button and it will start uploading the file in Analytics and queuing it in dataflow. Once done click on the **Got it** button.
10. Wait for 10-15 minutes (depending on the data, it may take a longer time to create the dataset).

9. Go to **Analytics Studio** and open the **DATASETS** tab. You can see the `Account_data` dataset as shown in the following screenshot:

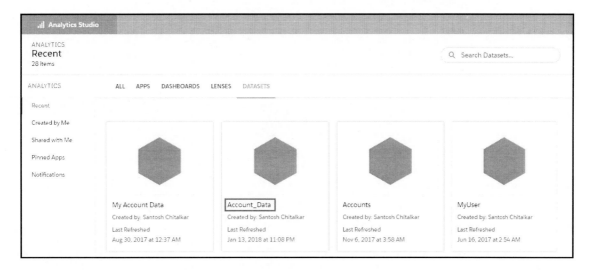

Congrats!!! You have created your first dataset.

Let's update this dataset with the same information but with some additional columns.

Updating datasets

We need to update the dataset to add new fields, change application settings, remove fields, and so on. Einstein Analytics gives users the flexibility to update the dataset. Here are the steps to update an existing dataset:

1. Create a CSV file to include some new fields and name it `Account_Data_Updated`.
2. Save the file to a location that you can easily remember.

3. In Salesforce, go to the **Analytics Studio** home page and find the dataset. Hover over the dataset and click on the ⌄ button, then click on **Edit**, as shown in the following screenshot:

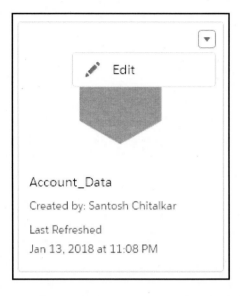

4. Salesforce displays the dataset editing screen. Click on the **Replace Data** button in the top-right corner of the page:

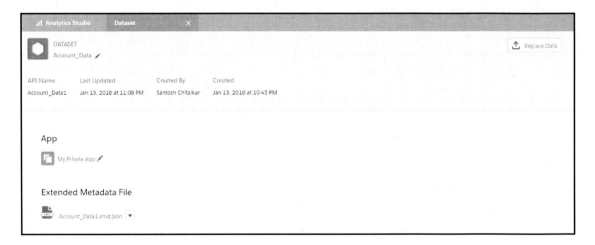

5. Click on the **Next** button and upload your new CSV file using upload UI.
6. Click on the **Next** button again to get to the next screen for editing and click on **Next** again.
7. Click on **Replace** as shown in the following screenshot:

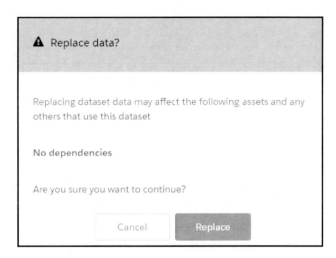

Creating your first dashboard

A dashboard is a pictorial representation of meaningful data put together in the form of charts, tables, images, and so on. It is a collection of multiple widgets that provide business insights using the dataset. It shows some relevant data/information from your dataset, which means you build your insights on datasets. The dashboard is required to clip your lenses. Let's take a look at the following steps for creating a dashboard:

1. In order to create a dashboard, click on **Create** and select **Dashboard**, as shown in the following screenshot:

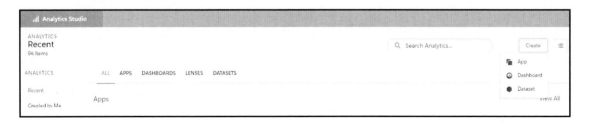

2. After you click on the **Dashboard** option, you should see the **Choose a dashboard template** window with some default dashboard templates. Salesforce provides default templates which you can choose from. Each template serves a different purpose. Here are some of the default templates:

- **Blank Dashboard in the Dashboard Designer**: This template creates a responsive dashboard with custom layouts for any device.
- **Comparison Dashboard**: This template compares the metrics side by side across a single dimension. It filters both columns of information using the filter bar.
- **Details Dashboard**: This template visualizes the data with record-level details in the table.
- **Summary Dashboard**: This template organizes the information into vertical sections with filters across top.
- **Three-Column Dashboard**: This template creates a dashboard with three columns and filters on top.
- **Tile Dashboard**: This template creates a home page for your application. It shows KPIs at the top with links to related child dashboards at the bottom.
- **Blank Dashboard in the Classic Designer**: This template creates a dashboard using the old designer.

Let's take a look at some of the preceding templates in the following screenshot:

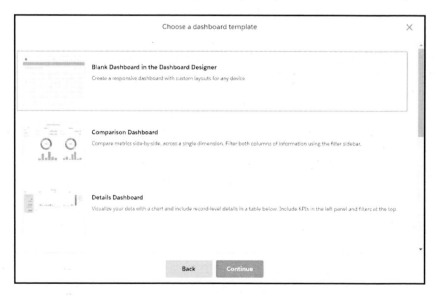

3. We will create our first dashboard, so select the **Blank Dashboard in the Dashboard Designer** template and click on **Continue**. Fill in the **Title** and **Description** fields and click on **Save**:

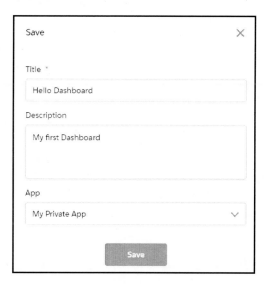

Go through the following screenshot and get familiar with your dashboard:

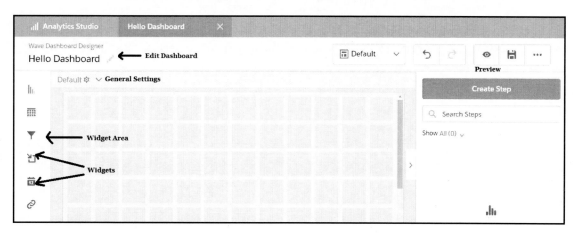

Creating lenses

Anutosh Infotech has millions of opportunity records in their database. They want to build a dashboard that will give them business insights into opportunity data. This dashboard should include the following charts and tables:

- A horizontal bar chart for opportunities closed in the current month and grouped by **Stage**. The chart should show the count of opportunities for each stage.
- A **Donut** chart for opportunities closed in the last month for each stage. The chart should display the sum of amount.
- A **Compare Table** for displaying **Owner Role** versus **Account Owner** displaying **Sum of Amount**.
- A **Stacked Bar** chart for the sum of opportunity amount, which is grouped by **Owner Role**, **Account Owner**, and **Stage**. The table should only show opportunities with **Stage Equals** to **Closed Won**, **Closed Lost**, or **Needs Analysis**.

Creating your first lens

A lens is a saved exploration that gives an insight into meaningful data. Let's create our first lens, to show data insights, by performing the following steps:

1. Go to **Analytics Studio I DATASETS**.
2. Search for the **DTC Opportunity** dataset and click on it. It should open a new tab called **New Lens** as shown in the following screenshot:

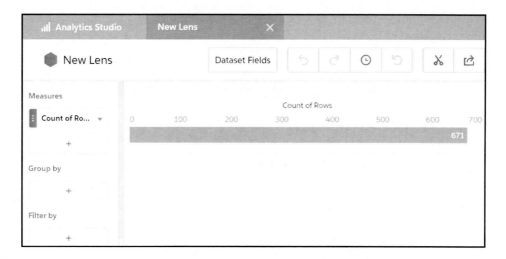

3. Click on the + button under the **Group by** section and select **Stage**, as shown in the following screenshot:

4. Click on the + button under the **Filter by** section and select **Close Date**. Click on the **Relative to now** tab; then click on **Months** and the **Add** button at the bottom, as shown in the following screenshot:

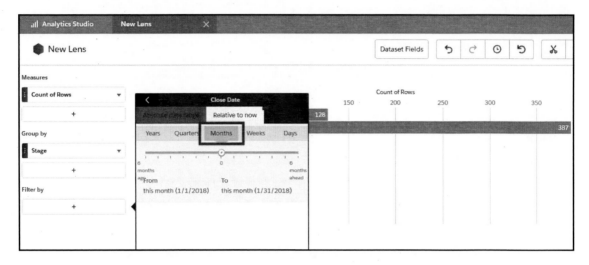

5. Click on the Save icon in the top-right corner to open a **Save** screen.

6. Name the lens title as `Hello Lens` and hit **Save**, as shown in the following screenshot:

Adding lenses to dashboards

A lens provides an insight into particular data. Users can do exploratory analysis and visualizations in lenses. For example, in millions of opportunity records, lenses might show only opportunities created this month in the **Bar** chart. Einstein Analytics provides simple point and click functionality to add lens to the dashboard. Let's add lens to our dashboards by performing the following steps:

1. Go to **Analytics Studio | DASHBOARDS.**
2. Clicking on `Hello Dashboard` and it will open it in a new tab.
3. Now click on **Analytics Studio** again and navigate to the **LENSES** tab.
4. Select the `Hello Lens` dataset you created earlier. It will open in the new tab.
5. Click on **Clip to Designer** or press *L* from the keyboard.
6. Enter `The Bar chart` under **Display Label**, as shown in the following screenshot:

7. Now go back to `Hello Dashboard`; you should see the **Create Step** option in the right-hand side panel list, as shown in the following screenshot:

8. Drag and drop the Chart widget into the dashboard.
9. Drag and drop the `The Bar chart` step into the widget.

Creating a Bar chart

As stated earlier, a user can add visualization to data insight. A user can integrate a step with many components such as a **Bar** chart, **Gauge** chart, Table, List, and so on. Let's create a **Bar** chart first by performing the following steps:

1. Navigate to **Trailhead Data Manager** | **Analytics Studio** | **DATASETS**.
2. Now click on the **Opportunity Details** dataset, which is created by default. After you click on the dataset, it will automatically open a new tab for **New Lens**. Go through the following screenshot and get familiar with your lens UI:

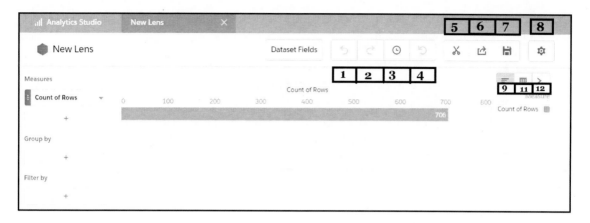

The tools numbered in the preceding screenshot are as follows:

1. Undo (z)
2. Redo (x)
3. View History
4. Reset
5. Clip to Designer (I)
6. Share (c)
7. Save (s)
8. Properties
9. Chart Mode
10. Table Mode
11. SAQL Mode

Let's explore some more features here:

- **Measure**: This is a quantitative value, such as the revenue and exchange rate. Measures are used for mathematical calculations such as maximum value, minimum value, sum, and so on.
- **Dimension**: This is a qualitative value, such as the type, stage, and product, and it is used for filtering data. You also use dimensions for grouping.
- **Filter**: This is used to get the required data only. It is a condition that processes the required data from the dataset.

The client wants an opportunity count for each stage. By default, **Measures** is set to **Count**. Now perform the following steps:

1. Edit the lens name/label to `Horizontal Bar Chart`
2. Add **Account Owner Role**, **Account Owner**, and **Stage**, respectively, by clicking on the plus sign under **Group by**
3. Add a filter for **Stage** and select **Closed Won**, **Closed Lost**, and **Needs Analysis**
4. Click on **Add**. After clicking on **Add**, you will get the following screenshot:

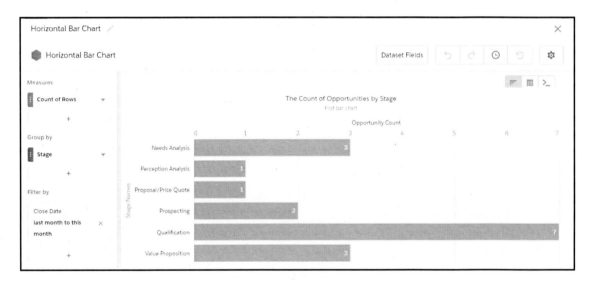

Select Count of Rows for Measures and Stage for Group in the lens properties.

5. Now click on **Properties**
6. Enter `The Count of Opportunities by Stage` under **Title** and `First bar chart` under **Subtitle**
7. Click on the **Bar Chart** option and change the **Auto fit** picklist value to **fit**
8. Click on **Y-Axis** and type `Stage Names` in the **Title** field
9. Click on **X-Axis (Top)** and type `Opportunity Count` in the **Title** field
10. Click on **Legend** and uncheck the **Show Legend** checkbox
11. Click on the **Done** button at the bottom of the screen

The following are some components where you can integrate lenses:

- **Chart**: This allows you to portray lens to **Bar** charts, **Stacked Bar** charts, **Pie** charts, and **Heat Map**. You can change how your chart is displayed by editing the widget settings.
- **Table**: Similar to lightning reports, you can set your step into a report format instead of a graphic, allowing you to delve into the details a little further.
- **List**: A filtering capability in Wave, a list will be set to your first grouping that you have set in place.
- **Number**: The Number widget represents total of the measure in the step. When filters are applied, this will be filtered to the selection(s) that is made by the viewer.
- **Toggle**: This allows you to toggle based on the **Groupings**, this can be set to **Single** or **Multi Select**, allowing you to filter data based on what you need to see.

You may say that's great, but what about the other components? And you're absolutely right, we should not limit functionality to about half of the components that are provided.

Whether you want to group specific components into a window, separate from others, or you have a deep desire to have a multicolored background, **containers** are your answer! Placing a container in the dashboard designer, you will be able to place other components on top of the container within its borders.

12. Save the lens as `Hello Lens2`

The Donut charts

A **Donut** or doughnut chart is nothing but a pie chart with a hole in the center. We can control the radius of the donut by using chart properties. **Donut** charts are more efficient and useful as they display critical information in slices. Let's perform the following steps to create a **Donut** chart:

1. Drag and drop the Chart widget into the dashboard and click on it.
2. Check the selected dataset. It should be **Opportunity Details**. If it is not the **Opportunity Details** dataset, then click on the **Back** button at the bottom and select the **Opportunity Details** dataset.

3. Edit the lens name/label to `Donut Chart`.
4. Add a **Sum** measure, select the **Amount** field, and remove the **Count of Rows** measure.
5. Select the **Owner Role** and **Stage** options under **Group by**.
6. Under **Filter by** add a filter for **Close Date** and select last month.
7. Click on **Done**. Take a look at the following screenshot depicting the **Donut** chart created after performing the preceding steps:

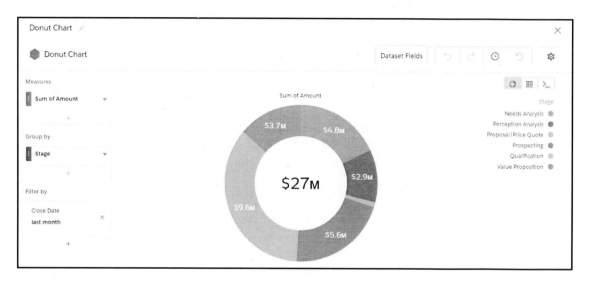

Compare Table

A compare table is an Excel sheet-like column-based visualization. We can add filters and measures to each column individually and, more importantly, we can create a column based on calculations. We can also add a maximum of four groupings in the table, that are applicable to all columns. Let's take a look at the following steps to create a compare table:

1. Drag and drop the Table widget into the dashboard and click on it.
2. Check the selected dataset. It should be the **Opportunity Details** dataset. If it is not the **Opportunity Details** dataset, then click on the **Back** button at the bottom and select the **Opportunity Details** dataset.

3. Edit the lens name/label to `Compare Table`.
4. Add **Measures** as **Sum**, select the **Amount** field, and remove the **Count of Rows** measure.
5. Select **Owner Role** and **Stage** under the **Group by** option.
6. Under **Filter by** add a filter for **Stage** and select **Closed Won**, **Closed Lost**, and **Needs Analysis**.
7. Click on Table Mode and select **Compare Table**.
8. Click on **Update**.

Take a look at the following screenshot depicting the **Compare Table**:

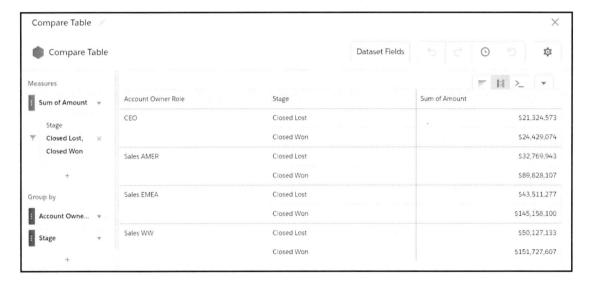

9. You should see a table on the dashboard; click on it. Navigate to **Properties** on the right-side panel.
10. Under the **TABLE PROPERTIES** option, click on **Column Width** and set the column width to **Fit to Widget**.
11. Click on **Update**.

Stacked Bar chart

A **Stacked Bar** chart gives you a simpler and easier way to compare values on the same bar. A single bar is segmented according to category. Different colors are used to show the different categories. Let's perform the following steps to create a **Stacked Bar** chart:

1. Drag and drop the **Chart** widget into the dashboard and click on it.
2. Check the selected dataset. It should be the **Opportunity Details** dataset. If it is not the **Opportunity Details** dataset, then click on the **Back** button at bottom and select the **Opportunity Details** dataset.
3. Edit the lens name to `Stacked Bar Chart`.
4. Click on the plus sign under **Measures**, and select **Sum**, and select the **Amount** field.
5. Add **Owner Role**, **Account Owner**, and **Stage**, respectively, using plus sign under **Group by**.
6. Add a filter for **Stage** and select **Closed Won**, **Closed Lost**, and **Needs Analysis**.
7. Click on **Done,** as shown in the following screenshot:

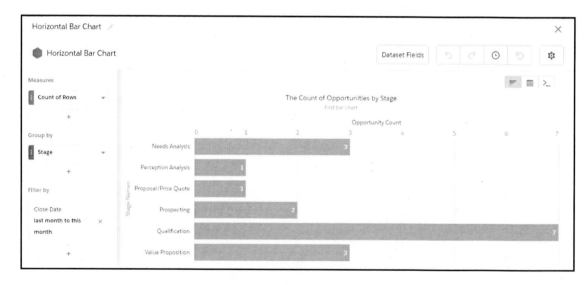

Select Count of Rows for Measures and Stage for Group in the lens properties.

You should see the horizontal **Bar** chart added on dashboard widget. Now click on the widget, go to its properties, and make the following changes to the settings:

1. Change the chart type to **Stacked Column**.
2. Click on **Properties**.
3. Enter `Stacked Column Bar` under **Title** and `Custom Action is here` under **Subtitle**.
4. Click on **Stacked Column Chart**, click on the **Auto fit** picklist, and set the value to **Fit**.
5. Scroll down to **X-Axis** and type `Grouped by Account Owner Role, Account Owner, and Stage` under **Title**. Also, set the size to **50%** to adjust **Account Owner**.
6. Click on **Legend** under **Position** and set the value to **bottom-center**.
7. Save the dashboard. Take a look at the following screenshot:

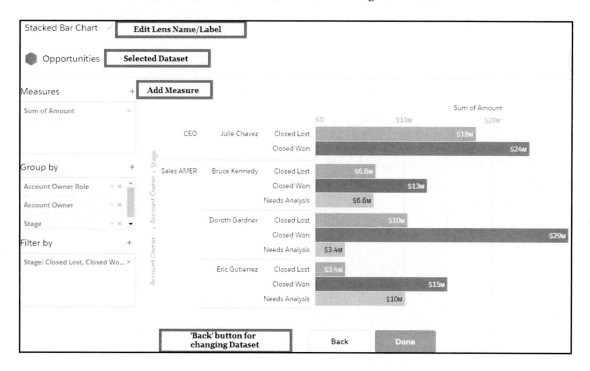

Dashboard customization

Einstein Analytics has a lot of features using which you can customize and design your dashboard by adding borders, background colors, and so on. Every component will allow you to set the border and background colors within the **WIDGET** tab along with determining if the component should be faceted or have global filters applied. If a component is faceted, it will connect to other faceted components and all the components will have the same filter applied to each of them. We will cover this in details in the next two chapter.

You can always preview a dashboard but keep in mind that Preview (e) does not mean save.

Creating your first Einstein Analytics application

Now that you have created your first dashboard, lens, chart, and table, Anutosh Infotech wants to create a few more dashboards. Also, they want to see all dashboards, lenses, and charts in a single folder so that they can view it in one go. So do we have any solution for them?

The answer is a big yes!!!

We can bundle all the components in a single application. So without wasting any time, let's create an Einstein Analytics application by performing the following steps:

1. On the **Analytics Studio** home page, click on the **Create** button and select **App**, as shown in the following screenshot:

2. Select the template for **Blank App** and click on **Continue**.

3. Enter the name of your application as `Hello App` and hit the **Create** button. Your application gets created, as shown in the following screenshot:

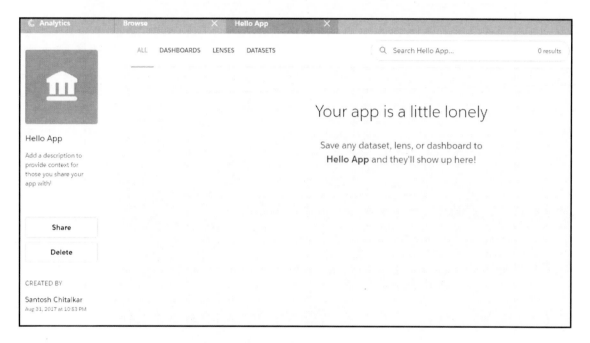

That was easy, wasn't it? Now let's add our `Hello Dashboard` dataset in our application.

4. Navigate to **Analytics Studio | DASHBOARDS**

5. Select the `Hello Dashboard` dashboard, which will open in a new tab.

6. Now click on Save and select `Hello App` from the **App** picklist.

7. Click on Save.

Take a look at the following screenshot:

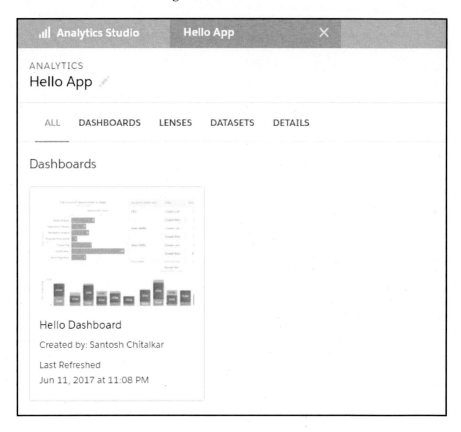

Set Smart Notification

Notification is a feature provided by Salesforce, that notifies you when you hit your targets. Einstein Analytics will work for you even if you are not on the Analytics platform. Einstein will analyze all your data and send notifications to you about your progress. You will receive the notification via email. You can track all your progress on the Analytics home page.

How do we set and manage notifications? Take a look at the following steps:

1. Go to **Analytics Studio** | **DASHBOARDS** and click on `Hello Dashboard`.
2. Click on Preview (e) or hit the *E* button on keyboard.
3. When you hover over **Compare Table**, you will see a drop-down arrow as shown in the following screenshot:

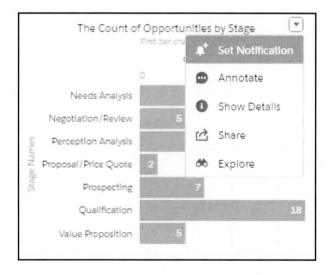

4. In the **New Notification** panel, set the value that you want to know about as soon as your widget query returns it. For example, say that you want to know when the **Stage** count has reached 16. You'd click on **Set Notification** on the **Compare Table**. In the **New Notification** panel, under **Notify me when the value**, you'd select **Equals or is greater than** from the drop-down list and enter 16 for the threshold value. Set the notification frequency. You can set the **Frequency** to **Every Weekday**, **Daily**, or **Weekly**. You can also set the time as shown in the following screenshot:

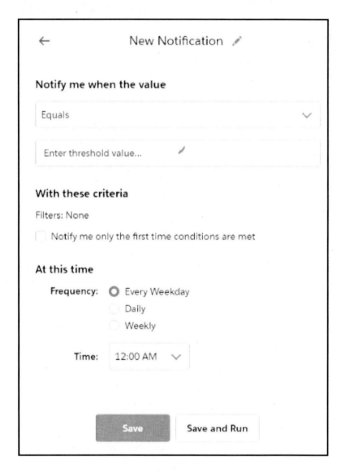

5. Click on **Save and Run**.

    When the conditions are met, you're notified in the application and via email. In Einstein, Lightning Experience, and Salesforce1, the bell icon (🔔) informs you of notifications. You can see the notification progress on the lower part of the Analytics home page. You can track progress as shown in the following screenshot:

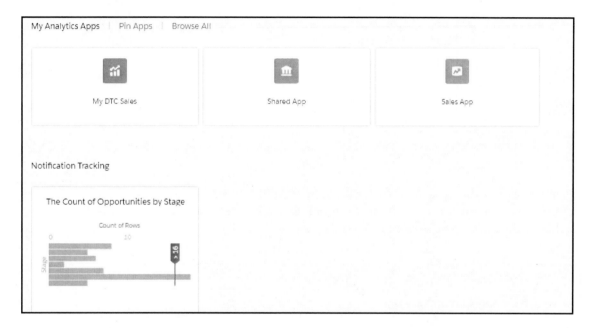

You can set notification from the drop-down list on any widget (except a timeline or values table).

You can create up to five notifications.

Keyboard shortcuts for Wave dashboards and lenses

In order to increase productivity, it is very important to know and use shortcuts. Einstein also provides multiple shortcuts that save a lot of time. Most shortcuts are the same in Windows and the Mac. The following are some common keyboard shortcuts:

Shortcuts for lens	Description
l ("L" lowercase)	Clip to Designer
S	Save
N	Clone in new tab
Ctrl + *E* (Windows) *cmd* + *E* (macOS)	Open JSON editor
D	Delete

Formatting your dashboard is always a time-consuming task. Einstein Analytics provides keyboards shortcuts for both Classic designer and Wave designer. If you are building a dashboard using Classic designer, the following keyboard shortcuts will save you a lot of time:

Shortcut for Classic designer	Description
Ctrl + Arrow keys (Windows) *cmd* + Arrow keys (macOS)	Move widgets by 1 pixel on dashboard
Ctrl + *Shift* + Arrow keys (Windows) *cmd* + Shift + Arrow keys (macOS)	Resize the widget by 1 pixel.
Arrow keys	Move widgets by 10 pixels on dashboard
Shift + Arrow keys	Resize the widget by 10 pixels.
[	Put the widget beneath other widgets.
]	Put the widget on top of other widgets
X	Delete the widget

If you are building a dashboard using Wave designer, use the following keyboard shortcuts:

Keyboard shortcuts for designer dashboard	Description
Arrow keys	Move the widget
Delete	Delete the selected widgets in the dashboard
C	Share the dashboard
D	Delete dashboard
E	Toggle between previewing or editing the dashboard
Q	Show clipped lenses or create a lens in the dashboard
R	Reset the dashboard to the last saved state
s	Save
x	Redo
z	Undo

If you are building a dashboard using JSON Editor, use the following keyboard shortcuts:

JSON Editor shortcuts	Description
Ctrl + *E* (Windows) *cmd* + *E* (macOS)	View dashboard with changes to JSON
Ctrl + *3* (Windows) *cmd* + *3* (macOS)	Disregard changes and load the original JSON
Ctrl + *F* (Windows) *cmd* + *F* (macOS)	Search (RegExp, case-sensitive, or whole-word searches available)
Ctrl + *F* twice (Windows) *cmd* + *F* twice (macOS)	Search and replace (RegExp, case-sensitive, or whole-word searches available)

Summary

Congratulations!!! We have successfully completed our third chapter. Now we know how to create datasets, lenses, and charts from it. We saw how to create a dashboard and add it to your application. We also covered setting up the notifications for important charts, updating the datasets, and configuring dashboards. In addition to all this, you learned about configuring and fine-tuning the charts.

In the next chapter, you will learn about data manager and dataflow. We will also explore dashboards in detail and see how to use all widgets and their settings.

We will also cover learning static step and custom actions.

4

Diving Deep into Einstein Analytics

In the previous chapter, we created our first dataset and dashboard. We also created our first lens, called `Hello Lens`, and we started building dashboards. In `Hello Dashboard`, we added a horizontal bar chart, and a donut chart using chart widgets. Now we understand the components in the widget area and adding lenses to charts. In this chapter, we are going to build a simple summary dashboard, and we will cover the following topics:

- Quota
- Dataflow and dataflow scheduling
- Data manager and setting
- Types of dashboard
- Declarative binding and faceting

Quota, dataflow, and data manager

A quota is the sales goal assigned to a user/rep (a business user) on a monthly or quarterly basis. It is important for representatives to achieve their quota on their own. It affects performance and hence it is important to understand quota attainment. The formula for quota attainment is as follows:

Quota Attainment = (Sales/quota)*100;

Which means if representatives/sales teams hit their goal by 60% then sales persons/users/representatives have a 40% quota attainment.

Creating a quota dataset

In order to create a CSV file for quotas, you need the following fields:

- StartDate (in yyyy-mm-dd format)
- QuotaAmount
- OwnerName
- Username

Let's take a look at the following code snippet, which depicts the preceding fields:

```
StartDate,QuotaAmount,OwnerName,Username
2017-01-07,5818,Julie Mcknight,santosh chitalkar
2017-01-07,5818,Brandon Hough,santosh chitalkar
2017-01-07,5818,Stephanie Alexander,santosh chitalkar
2017-01-03,4200,Robin Vachhani,santosh chitalkar
2017-01-03,4200,Paul Speisman,santosh chitalkar
2017-01-03,4200,Jennifer Sampson,santosh chitalkar
2017-01-03,4200,Janice Parsons,santosh chitalkar
2017-01-03,4200,Shane Paquette,santosh chitalkar
2017-01-03,4200,Ashleigh Farrell,santosh chitalkar
2017-01-02,5818,Rachel Walton,santosh chitalkar
2017-01-02,5818,Chris Thomas,santosh chitalkar
2017-01-02,5818,Renee Rountree,santosh chitalkar
2017-01-02,5818,Glenn Nakamura,santosh chitalkar
2017-01-02,5818,Nate Fletcher,santosh chitalkar
2017-01-01,2909,Jackson Morgan,santosh chitalkar
2017-01-01,5818,Renae Dotson,santosh chitalkar
2017-01-01,7350,Kim Thomas,santosh chitalkar
2017-01-01,7350,Mary Obot,santosh chitalkar
2017-01-01,7350,Jay Lyonett,santosh chitalkar
2017-01-07,7350,Jane LaBonte,santosh chitalkar
2017-01-06,7350,George Benson,santosh chitalkar
```

 The quota field names should be exactly the same as they are case-sensitive.

Let's take a look at the following steps for creating a quota dataset:

1. Navigate to **Create | Dataset**.
2. In the **New Dataset** window, enter First_Quota under **Dataset Name** and select Hello App in the **App** field.

3. Click on **Next** as shown in the following screenshot:

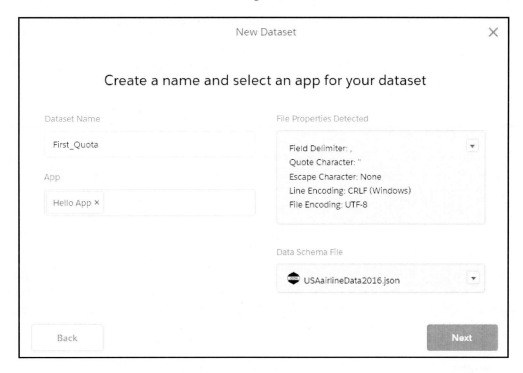

4. After you click on the **Next** button, Einstein uses the dataflow to create a dataset.
5. Navigate to `Hello App` and select the **DATASETS** tab. You should see that the `First_Quota` dataset has been created

Dataflows in Einstein Analytics

A dataflow is used to create one or more dataset from data pulled from Salesforce or an external system.

A dataflow transforms the dataset in such a way that it can be available to query and build lenses.

Dataflow

A dataflow is used to pull data from resources and bring it into the Einstein platform. It is really important to understand dataflow design and the terms used in it as the dataflow decides which data to pull and which needs to be available for queries. Here are some concepts used.

Transformations

This is the manipulation of data. Transformations can be added to datasets, Salesforce objects, and external data. We can merge different datasets together and create a new dataset by using transformation. There are many types of transformation, including `sfdcDigest`, `sfdcRegister`, `augment`, `append`, and so on.

augment

As the name suggests, this transformation joins columns of different datasets to make a new dataset, and this new augmented dataset can be used for querying.

Each dataset can be related to every other one by defining the left key and right key.

For example, in `account` and `contact` as shown in the following code snippet:

```
"left_key": [ "Id" ],"right_key": [ "AccountId" ]
```

sfdcDigest

The sfdcDigest concept is used to generate datasets. In the sfdcDigest action attribute, we can define the fields and objects that we want to extract from Salesforce. We can also add filter conditions here (though it is not required) as follows:

```
"action":"sfdcDigest",
"parameters":{
    "Object":"Account",
    "fields":[
        {
            "name":"Id"
        },
        {
            "name":"Name"
        },
        {
            "name":"OwnerId"
        },
        {
            "name":"AccountSource"
        },
        {
            "name":"Type"
        },
        {
            "name":"Industry"
        },
        {
            "name":"BillingCountry"
        },
        {
            "name":"BillingState"
        },
        {
            "name":"CreatedDate"
        },
        {
            "name":"LastModifiedDate"
        }
    ],
    "object":"Account"
    }
},
```

sfdcRegister

The `sfdcRegister` attribute is used to make the dataset available for queries. So, `sfdcRegister` registers the created dataset. If the dataset is not registered under `sfdcRegister`, the user cannot view it and cannot query it:

```
"101":{
    "action":"sfdcDigest",
    "parameters":{
        "fields":[
            {
                "name":"Name"
            },
            {
                "name":"IsProfilePhotoActive"
            },
            {
                "name":"LastName"
            },
            {
                "name":"Id"
            }
        ],
        "object":"User"
    }
},
"102":{
    "action":"sfdcRegister",
    "parameters":{
        "name":"MyUser",
        "alias":"MyUser",
        "source":"101"
    }
},
```

Required permissions

In order to create a new dataflow, the user must have the **Edit Wave Analytics** permission. As we have already assigned a permission set to the user, they should have the **Edit Wave Analytics** permission.

Let's take a look at the following steps:

1. To verify, switch to Classic mode, then navigate to **Setup** | **Administer** | **Manage Users** | **Users** and select your user:

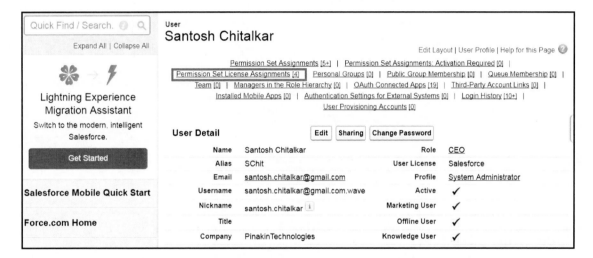

2. Navigate to **Permission Set License Assignments** | **Edit Assignments** and confirm that **Edit Wave Analytics permission** is not there, then edit the permission set and select it.

3. Next, we need to enable replication by clicking on **Setup**. In **Quick Find / Search...** type `Analytics` and click on **Settings**, as shown in the following screenshot:

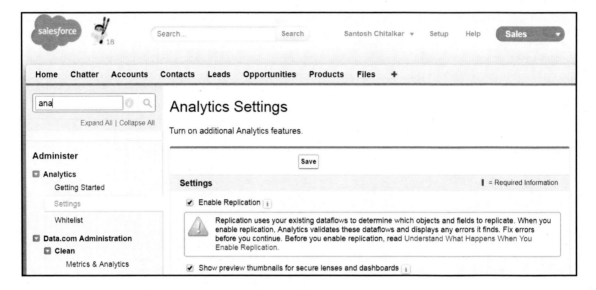

4. Select the **Enable Replication** option and click on **Save**.

Configuring a dataflow

Now that we have enabled replication, let's go back to our Einstein Analytics environment. Our next step is to go to the data monitor:

1. On your right-hand side, in the top corner, you should see the settings icon; click on it and open **Data Manager**:

2. After you click on **Data Manager**, it will open a **Data Manager** page in a new browser tab:

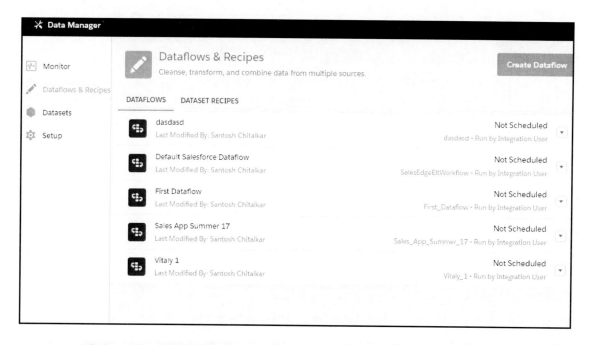

3. Click on **Dataflows & Recipes** from the left-hand side panel and you should see a **Create Dataflow** button in the top-right corner.

4. Click on **Create Dataflow** and enter `First Dataflow` as the name of your dataflow:

5. Click on **Monitor** and select **Dataflow View** as shown in the following screenshot:

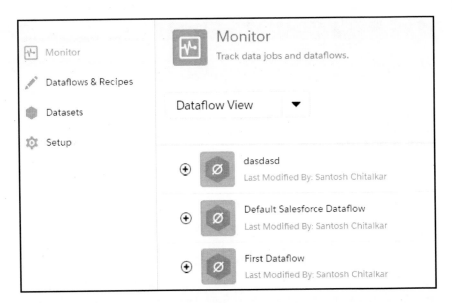

6. To download the dataflow definition file, click on **Download** in the actions list:

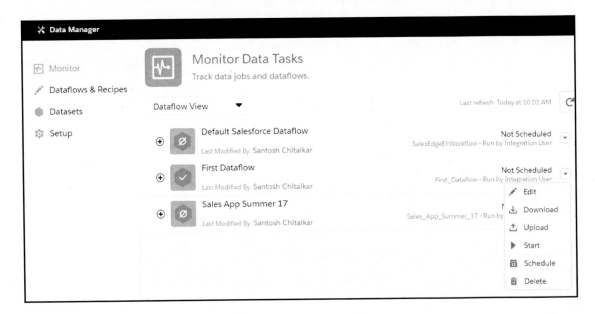

7. As we just created our dataflow, the downloaded file will have nothing in it except { }. Edit that file and add the following transformation to it and save it:

```
{
    "Extract_Opportunity":{
        "action":"sfdcDigest",
        "parameters":{
            "fields":[
                {
                    "name":"Id"
                },
                {
                    "name":"Name"
                },
                {
                    "name":"Amount"
                },
                {
                    "name":"AccountId"
                }
            ],
            "object":"Opportunity"
        }
    },
    "Register_OpportunityDetails":{
        "action":"sfdcRegister",
        "parameters":{
            "alias":"My_Dataflow_Oppty",
            "name":"My_Dataflow_Oppty",
            "source":"Extract_Opportunity"
        }
    }
}
```

8. Go to the action list and click on **Upload**.
9. Select the file from your local system and click on **Upload**.
10. Click on **Done**.

Dataflow

Dataflow does not create a column for null columns, which means source data should have at least one non-null value in the column. By default, the dataflow runs daily.

Einstein Analytics

Einstein Analytics automatically registers datasets created by uploading external data.

Running a dataflow

Now that you have successfully created a dataflow, you need to run it manually. The dataflow fetches the data from Salesforce; After you run the dataflow, it brings new/updated data into Einstein Analytics. The dataflow does not run automatically; you need to run it manually for the first time. Once it has run manually then it will run automatically on a daily basis. The following are the steps to run a dataflow:

1. Open **Data Manager** and click on **Data Monitor**.
2. By default, **Jobs View** is selected; change this to **Dataflow View**.
3. You should see all your dataflows here. Click on the actions list for the desired dataflow.
4. Click on **Start** to start running a dataflow.
5. You will receive a success or failure notification via email after the job is complete.

6. Now, click on **DATASETS** and check for the dataset. It should have created a new dataset, My_Dataflow_Oppty, as shown in the following screenshot:

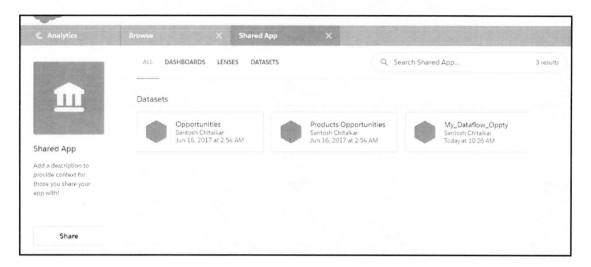

Scheduling the dataflow

It is very important for any business to have updated data to make relevant calculations and business decisions. Once you have run a dataflow manually, it runs daily. We can schedule the dataflow to run at particular times as per our requirements. Einstein offers an easy point and click feature to schedule your dataflow. Just perform the following steps and schedule your dataflow to ensure your data:

1. From Einstein Analytics, go to **Data Manager**.
2. Select **Dataflow View**.

3. Click on the action list and select **Schedule**:

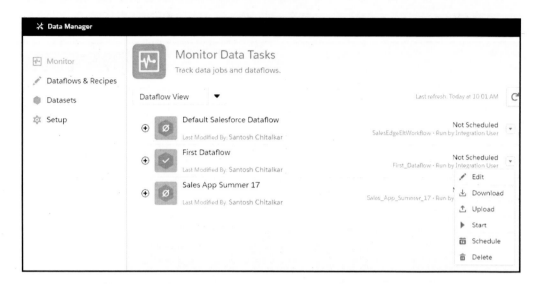

4. A time dialog box opens. You can schedule your job on an **Hour**, **Week**, or **Month** basis. Select your chosen time and day, and click on **Save**:

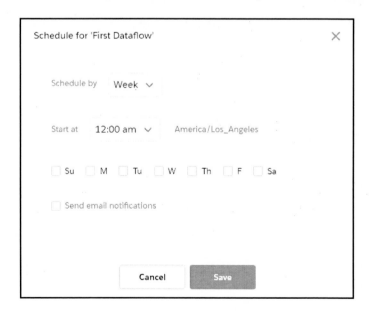

Einstein dashboards

An Einstein dashboard is a collection of your charts, tables, and maps. It is a collection of widgets that give you useful business insights.

You can design your dashboard in either of the following two ways:

- Wave Dashboard Designer
- Classic Designer

Differences between Wave Dashboard Designer and Classic Designer

Wave Dashboard Designer	Classic Designer
You can design layouts for different devices using the UI.	No UI is provided for mobile layouts. You have to use JSON.
You can create steps within the dashboard.	You have to clip the step to dashboard.
Supports annotations and notifications.	Doesn't support annotations and notifications.
Single-table widget for **Compare Table**, **Value Table**, and **Pivot Table**.	Different widgets for different tables.
You can hide steps.	Cannot hide steps.
You can build advanced dashboards.	You can build basic dashboards.

Creating a dashboard using Wave Dashboard Designer

To create an Einstein dashboard using Wave Dashboard Designer, perform the following steps:

1. Navigate to **Analytics Studio | Create | Dashboard**
2. Select the **Summary Dashboard** template and click on **Continue**
3. Enter `Einstein Summary Dashboard` under **Name your dashboard**, and select `Hello App`
4. Click on **Create**

It will automatically create a summary layout along with empty widgets.

The General option under LAYOUT settings

Einstein Wave Dashboard Designer provides the flexibility of updating the dashboard's properties, such as by adding columns, changing the background color, cell spacing, and so on.

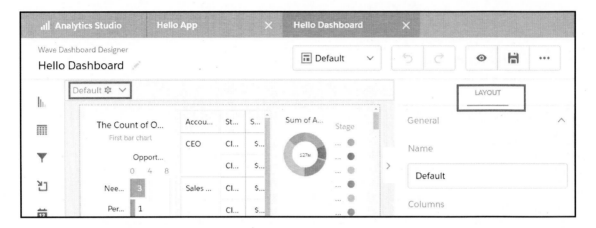

To change the properties, click on gear icon ⚙ and change the following settings:

1. Increase **Columns** to **50** by clicking on the + button. **50** is the maximum number of columns which you can add.
2. Set **Row Height** to **Fine**.
3. Set **Cell Spacing** to **0** for both **Horizontal** and **Vertical**.
4. Change the background color and adjust the dashboard layout to full length.
5. Save the dashboard.

Displaying the top 10 opportunities in the Bar chart

Bar charts are a very important visualization which use bars for comparing data between categories. We can use either a vertical or a horizontal bar chart, and the longer the bar the more the value. We are going to use Bar chart to display the top 10 opportunities by performing the following steps:

1. Click on the empty **Bar** chart widget in the first section.
2. Edit the step label by clicking on **Clip to Designer (I)** and enter `Top 10 Oppty` under **Display Label**.
3. Add **Sum** under **Measures** and select the **Amount** field.
4. Click on the down arrow for **Sum of Amount** under **Measures** and select ↓ **Sort descending,** as shown in the following screenshot:

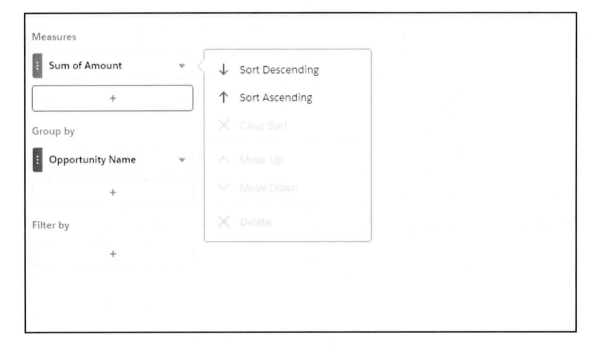

5. Choose **Opportunity Name** under **Group by**.
6. Switch to **SAQL Mode** and limit it to `10`.

7. Click on **Run Query** and see the result. Your SAQL should look as follows:

```
q = load "opportunity";
q = group q by 'Name';
q = foreach q generate 'Name' as 'Name', sum('Amount') as
'sum_Amount';
q = order q by 'sum_Amount' desc;
q = limit q 10;
```

8. Save the result.

Einstein adds this step to the panel, and you can reuse the same step for different widgets. Now, let's change the properties of our Bar chart. To do this, click on **WIDGET**, and the widget property section will appear on the right-side panel. Let's perform the following steps:

1. Enter `Top 10 Opportunities` in the **Section Title** field and `By Amount` in the **Subtitle** field.
2. Change the chart type to the **Column** chart.
3. Click on the **Column Chart** section and check the **Bin Values** checkbox. You can add low and high values under the **Low Value** and **High Value** options, along with color coding.
4. Click on **Y-axis (Left)** and uncheck **Show title**.
5. Click on **Legend**, and under **Position** change the position to **bottom-center**.
6. Click on **Update**.
7. Save your dashboard and click on Preview (e):

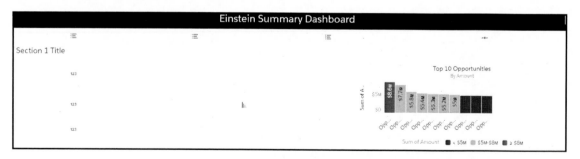

The bar chart for the top 10 Opportunities is displayed at the right of the dashboard

Donut charts for the top five opportunity owners

The first chart in the dashboard we created displays the top 10 opportunities, along with amounts. Now, we are going to create a pie chart for the top five opportunity owners by amount, by performing the following steps:

1. Click on the second empty chart widget in the first section
2. Edit the step name to `Top 5 Oppty Owner`
3. Add **Sum** under **Measures**, and select the **Amount** field
4. Select **Opportunity Owner** under **Group by**, and switch to **SAQL Mode**
5. Change the limit to 5, as shown in the following code snippet:

```
q = load "opportunity";
q = group q by 'Owner.UniqueUserName';
q = foreach q generate 'Owner.UniqueUserName' as
'Owner.UniqueUserName', sum('Amount') as 'sum_Amount';
q = order q by 'Owner.UniqueUserName' asc;
q = limit q 5;
```

6. Click on **WIDGET** and change the chart to the **Donut** chart from the **WIDGET** properties panel
7. Click on Properties
8. In the **CHART PROPERTIES** panel, click on the **Donut Chart** section and uncheck **Show measure title**
9. Click on **Done**
10. Save the dashboard

Adding numbers for KPI

Number widgets are the best widgets for showing the **key performance indicator** (KPI). KPIs are very important for displaying critical calculations. Unlike chart widgets, number widgets require at least one measure, and a number widget requires a step that has at least one measure.

 Steps for number widgets can have multiple measures as well, and Einstein provides the flexibility to choose which measure you want to display.

Let's create a KPI for quota to display the total quota amount, by performing the following steps:

1. Click on the empty **Number** widget on your dashboard.
2. The **Choose Dataset** screen appears. By default, the most recently used dataset appears on top. Select the dataset in the **Create Step** tab.
3. Click **Untitled Step** and enter the step label as `Quota Amount`.
4. Add **Measures** as **Sum** and select the `QuotaAmount` field.
5. Click on **Done**.
6. Change the **WIDGET** and **STEP** properties by selecting the widget.
7. Change the title to `Quota Amount`, and check the **shorten number** checkbox. The **shorten number** checkbox simplifies the display of values by rounding it; for example, 1,000 is displayed as 1k, 1,000,000 as 1M, and so on.
8. You can also change the text size and color from step general properties:

Closed Won and Closed Lost opportunity amounts

Let's add the total amount for **Closed Won** opportunities by performing the following steps:

1. Click on the second number widget and select the **Opportunity** dataset. If the **Opportunity** dataset is not selected, click on the **Back / Change Dataset** button and select the **Opportunity** dataset.
2. Change the step label to **Closed Won**.
3. To get the total amount for opportunities, add **Measures** as **Sum** and select the **Amount** field.
4. Under **Filter by** add the filter for **Stage**, **Equals** to **Closed Won**.
5. Click on **Done**.
6. Change the properties to shorten the number.
7. Now click on **WIDGET** and clone the widget from the step action.

8. Change the step label to `Closed Lost` and change the filter criterion to **Stage**, **Equals** to **Closed Lost**.
9. Click on **Done** and drag and drop the step from the **STEP** panel to the third widget in the dashboard canvas.

Listing widgets by Opportunity Type, Role Name, and Opportunity Owner

A **List** widget is a filter widget that gives the flexibility of filtering dashboard data to the user. Users can filter dashboard results based on a dimension. We are going to build three steps for a **List** widget using **Opportunity Type**, **Role Name**, and **Opportunity Owner**, and this will change the dashboard results based upon the value selection.

When we create a step for a **List** widget, it is important to have a single-grouping dimension. Grouped values appear in the list.

Take a look at the following screenshot depicting the **Einstein Summary Dashboard**:

In the **Einstein Summary Dashboard** layout, you can see three **List** widgets and one **Range** widget in one row.

Let's take a look at the following steps:

1. To open the wizard, click the button inside the first **List** widget
2. Select the **Opportunity** dataset
3. To use a different dataset, click on **Change Dataset**
4. Select the **Account_Type** field
5. Click on **Create**

6. Preview the dashboard and click on the **List** widget, as shown in the following screenshot:

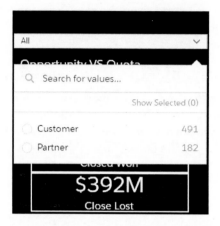

Owner Role Name and Opportunity Owner lists

Let's create a second and third list filter for **Role Name** and **Opportunity Owner**. We can use this to filter the dashboard based on role and owner selection:

1. To open the wizard, click the button inside the second list widget.
2. Select the **Opportunity** dataset.
3. To use a different dataset, click on **Change Dataset**.
4. Select the **Owner_Role** field.
5. Click on **Create**. Take a look at the following screenshot:

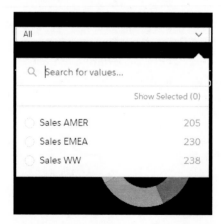

6. Repeat the same steps till *step 3*, and on *step 4* select the **Account_Owner** field to create a list. Your widget will look as shown in the following screenshot:

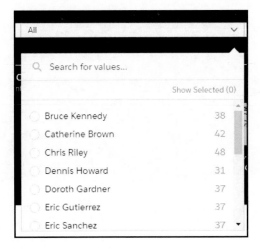

7. Save the dashboard and click on Preview (e).

The Range filter widget

The **Range** widget is again used to filter a dashboard based on a range of data. This range can be either a date or a number. Let's create an amount range filter.

1. To open the wizard, click the button inside the second list widget.
2. Select the **Opportunity** dataset.
3. To use a different dataset, click on **Change Dataset**.
4. Select the **Amount** field.
5. Click on **Create** and save the dashboard:

6. Preview your dashboard and change the values in your list filter. All the widgets/lenses on your dashboard will update on the list filter, as shown in the following screenshot:

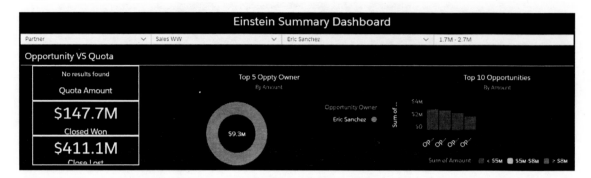

You might be wondering, how is this happening and what is the connection? How the dashboard is updating to list filter?

The answer is **faceting**. All the widgets are connected to each other because they are from the same dataset, and connected through the facet option.

If you don't want to update a particular widget upon list value selection, you can remove the faceting. Let's say, for instance, that in our dashboard we don't want the KPI section (all number widgets) to update on list selection; we can then add/remove faceting by performing the following simple steps:

1. Open our dashboard in edit mode and click on the **Closed Won** widget
2. In the **STEP** properties panel, click on the **STEP** tab
3. Now, you can see two checkboxes, **Facet** and **Apply global filters**
4. Uncheck the **Facet** checkbox
5. Repeat this for the remaining two number widgets
6. Save the dashboard and preview it
7. Now, select the value from the **Account_Type** list, and notice that upon selection the dashboard updates (except for the KPI section) as shown in the following screenshot:

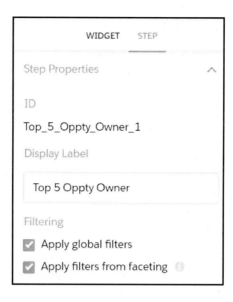

What is faceting?

Faceting is the easiest and fastest way to connect widgets on a dashboard. All faceted components on the dashboard can interact with each other. When we facet steps, all the dashboard widgets update upon selecting the Chart, Toggle, Range, or List widget. Selecting one widget results in filtering all other faceted widgets.

This is certainly is the easiest and fastest way to connect all dashboard components, but it is very limited. Facet options only work for components/widgets of the same dataset. That's why you can see that the Quota Amount widget doesn't respond to list selection even though the **Facet** option is selected. We can connect widgets from two different datasets by using the connect datasource feature.

By default, steps in the same datasets are faceted.

Connecting datasources

This feature is also called **declarative binding**, as it has a declarative interface through which we can connect two different datasets. We are already aware that steps of the same dataset can filter each other's data automatically via the facet feature. However, faceting cannot be used in this case, as there are two different datasets involved. In order to facet steps from two different datasets, we can use an Einstein feature called **data resources**. Data resources can be used to connect two dataset steps, but they should have a common value column. Let's connect **Quota** and **Opportunity** with each other. Both datasets have a common column called **Owner_Name** which can be used to connect them with each other.

Let's take a look at the following steps:

1. Click on the three dots and select **Connect Data Sources**, as shown in the following screenshot:

2. Click on **New Connection** and enter `Quota_Oppty_connection` in the **Connection Name** field
3. Select **Data Source 1** as `First_Quota`, and select the **OwnerName** field

4. Select **Data Source 2** as opportunity and select the field called **Owner.Name**, as shown in the following screenshot:

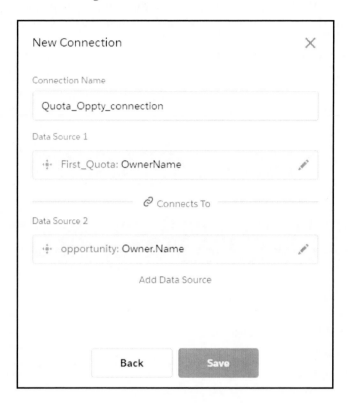

5. Click on **Save**
6. Preview the dashboard and change the **Owner.Name** list value
7. You can see that Quota Amount updates upon list value selection

Setting initial values to filters

In the **Einstein Summary Dashboard**, when the dashboard is in preview mode, we can see that all the filter widget values are set to all. However, if we want to set a default value on load, we can use **Pick Initial Selections**. Use the following steps to set initial values:

1. Open the dashboard in edit mode
2. Click on the three dots and then select **Pick Initial Selections**
3. After clicking on this, the dashboard will automatically go to preview mode, where you can select initial values for all filters on the dashboard
4. Click on **Done**
5. You can use the same method to set default values to the static step as well

Creating a dashboard using Classic Designer

Classic Designer is an efficient way of creating basic dashboards in Einstein Analytics. To create a dashboard using Classic Designer, perform the following few steps:

1. Navigate to **Analytics Studio | Create | Dashboard**.
2. It will open a layout template; scroll down till the end and select **Blank Dashboard in Classic Designer**.
3. Click on **Continue**.
4. If you are opening this template for the first time, a pop-up window will appear. Select **Not now** and save the dashboard to `Hello App`:

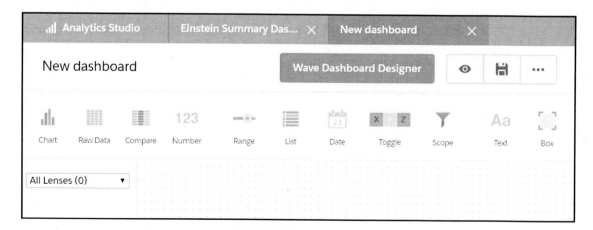

At first glance, we can see that there are some key differences between Classic and Wave Dashboard Designer. Unlike Wave Dashboard Designer, we cannot see a direct button to create steps here, and the **STEP** panel is on the left-hand side. All the widgets are provided on the top row. Also, there are two separate table widgets.

Creating your first chart in Classic Designer

Unlike Wave Designer, you don't need to drag and drop widgets in the dashboard canvas. Widgets will automatically be added onto the canvas after clicking on them. So, without further ado, let's start creating our first chart:

1. To add a new widget to the dashboard canvas, click on the **Chart** widget
2. Go to **Analytics Studio** and click on **DATASETS**
3. Select the **Opportunity** dataset and click on it
4. It will open a new lens in a new tab
5. Add **Measure** as **Average** and select the field as **Amount**
6. Add the **Billing Country** field under **Group by** and under **Filter by**, **Close Date**, **Equals** this quarter
7. Click on the **Add** button
8. Clip the lens and enter the label `Avg amount by Country`
9. Go to your dashboard, and you should see the lenses in the **Lens** panel
10. Now, select the widget and then click on **Lens**
11. It will be added on the widget
12. Save the dashboard

Donut charts for Opportunities by Industry

Let's create a donut chart to display the amount per industry by performing the following steps:

1. Repeat the first four steps of the first dashboard, and click on the **Opportunity** dataset.
2. It will open a new lens. Add **Sum** as **Measures** and select the **Amount** field.
3. Select **Industry** under **Group by** and clip the step to designer.
4. Go to dashboard and click on Chart widget.
5. Make sure that your newly added widget is selected, and then click on your step.
6. Change the type to **Donut** chart.

Funnel chart for Opportunities by Stage

Let's create a donut chart to display the amount on each stage by performing the following steps:

1. Repeat the first four steps for the first dashboard, and click on the **Opportunity** dataset.
2. It will open a new lens. Add the **Sum of Amount** measure to it.
3. Select **Stage** under **Group by** and clip the step to the designer.
4. Go to the dashboard and click on the Chart widget.
5. Make sure that your newly added widget is selected, and then click on your step.
6. Change the type to **Funnel** chart as shown in the following screenshot:

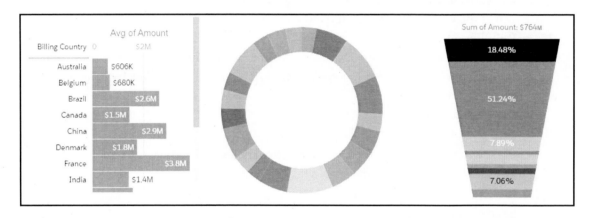

Converting your dashboard to a Wave Dashboard Designer

As we can clearly see, the Classic Designer is quicker but a basic canvas. We can convert this dashboard to a Wave dashboard by clicking on the **Wave Dashboard Designer** button. By converting it to Wave dashboard, we can use the advanced features of the Wave dashboard. When you click on the **Wave Dashboard Designer** button, it converts a Classic Designer Dashboard to a Wave Designer Dashboard, and saves it as a copy of the original:

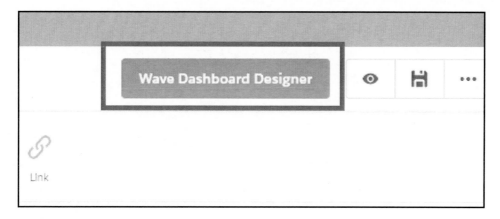

Classic and Wave Designer both use different runtime engines, and both have different syntax, so certain elements may not work properly; these elements you will need to change manually.

Summary

In this chapter, we learned how to upload a quota and create a dataset. Dataflows are used to create one or more datasets. We also saw how to schedule the dataflow, and covered how to build our dashboard using either Wave Dashboard Designer or Classic Designer; Wave Dashboard Designer is an advanced dashboard canvas. We also saw that Einstein Analytics provides pre-built dashboard templates. We have created an `Einstein Summary Dashboard` dashboard using the **Summary Dashboard** template, and we can use dashboards and general widget properties to customize them.

In the next chapter, we will cover bindings in Einstein, static step, custom actions, how to set up Sales Cloud Einstein, and how to build an executive dashboard for a sales team.

5
Einstein for Sales

We are now familiar with two types of dashboard designer that we can use to create dashboards: Classic Designer and Wave Dashboard Designer. Faceting and connected data sources are the two point and click binding functionalities provided by Einstein to connect different components on a dashboard. But these two features are limited. This chapter covers selection and result binding, which gives more flexibility to users in making dashboard components interact with each other. We are also going to enable Sales Cloud Einstein and go through the built-in dashboards it provides.

This chapter is completely practical. We are going to cover the following topics:

- Creating an executive dashboard
- Static step
- Selection and result binding
- Setting up Sales Cloud Einstein

Executive dashboard for a sales team

Anutosh Infotech wants to build an executive dashboard so that they can see their company performance, KPIs, important information, and other details in one dashboard. The following is a mockup diagram of their requirements:

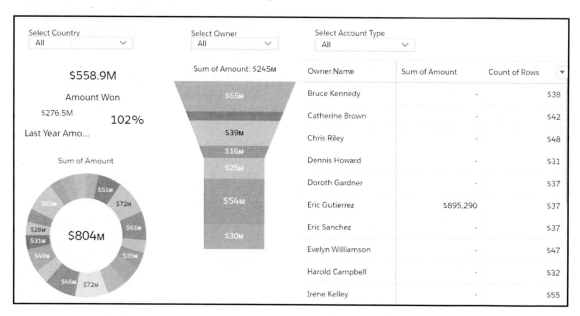

Now that we have our requirements, let's start building our dashboard.

In order to create the dashboard, perform the following steps:

1. First, we need to create all of the required datasets
2. Create the `Opportunity` and `Account` datasets
3. After we have all of the required datasets, create a blank dashboard and name it `Executive dashboard for Sale`
4. Go to the dashboard **LAYOUT** settings and change the **Columns** to **50**
5. Change **Row Height** to **Fine** and set **Cell Spacing** to **0** for both **Horizontal** and **Vertical**, as shown in the following screenshot:

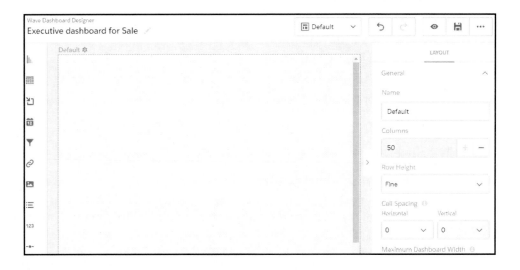

Expected revenue KPIs

As per the client's requirements, we need to create a KPI for the actual revenue, potential revenue, and actual target achieved. We need to use a number of widgets for all KPIs here.

Actual revenue earned

This KPI should show the **Sum of Amount** measure for the **Closed Won** opportunities. Wave Dashboard Designer provides a direct option to create this. The following are the steps you'll need to perform:

1. Go to the right-side panel and click on **Create Step** as shown in the following screenshot:

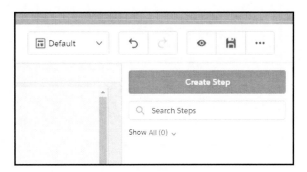

2. Name the step `Actual closed won`
3. Set the **Measures** as **Sum** and select the **Amount** field
4. Set the **Filter by** field as **Close Date**
5. Go to the **Relative to now** option and select **Years**; choose the current year
6. Also add a filter for the field **Won** as **true**
7. Click on **Done**

Now, let's fine-tune the widgets by using general settings. Perform the following steps:

1. Select the checkbox **Shorten number**.
2. Repeat the preceding steps to create our second lens for the last/previous year; or select the number widget, go to the **Step Action** option at the bottom, and clone the step.
3. Change the filter condition for the **Close Date** field to last year. Rename this step `Actual closed Won Prior`.
4. Add a second number widget to the dashboard and drop the `Actual closed Won Prior` step on it. Fine-tune this numerical widget by performing the following steps:
   1. Remove the title
   2. Set the **Shorten number** checkbox as **true**
   3. In the **Text Style** section, set the number **Size** to **16**, and under **Alignment**, select **Center**
5. Now add the third widget to the dashboard, which is the Text widget. Add the following text: `Last Year Amount`. Fine-tune and adjust these three widgets as shown in the following screenshot:

The static step

Einstein Analytics is a very powerful tool that gives a lot of functionality to users. But grouping, filtering, selecting measures, and so on are usually all done by admins only. If we can make our dashboard flexible enough to let users choose the grouping and filtering, then it really is an awesome feature. So can we do this in Einstein? Is it possible?

The answer is yes; it is possible, and a static step is the way to achieve it. Static steps are a way for you to empower this flexibility.

So let's create our static step by performing the following steps:

1. Click on **Create Step**
2. Click on **Create a Static Step with Custom Values**
3. Enter **Display Label** as Static_Country and add country values as shown in the following screenshot:

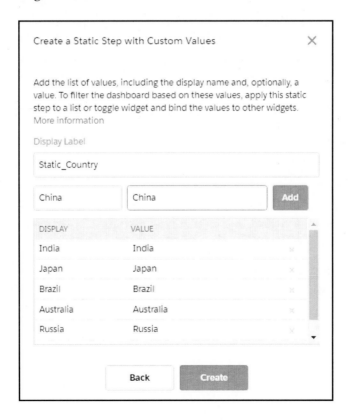

You can add other countries as well

4. Click on **Create** and add a List widget to the dashboard
5. Drag and drop our country static step onto the list
6. Click on Preview (e)

Take a look at the following screenshot:

Bindings in Einstein

In our `Executive dashboard for Sale` dashboard, we have KPIs and static steps. KPIs can interact with each other by faceting as they are from the same dataset. What if we connect static steps and KPIs together? We can do this using **bindings**.

Binding is a way to make components on dashboards communicate with each other. Bindings between components result in updating related components upon selection.

The following are two types of binding:

- Selection binding
- Result binding

Binding can be used in both the Wave and Classic Designer Dashboards. Both dashboards treat selection and results differently.

Selection binding

Selection binding results in updating a step after the selection of another step. For example, in our dashboard, if we use selection binding between the `Static_Country` step and KPIs, then after selecting a value from the `Static_Country` step it will update the KPI values. After selecting any value from the widget, it will re-evaluate all connected steps.

Einstein Analytics provides three main types of function; data selection, data manipulation, and data serialization.

Data selection functions

Data selection functions are used to select data from the source table/step/result. Data selection functions are further divided into cell functions, column functions, and row functions as follows:

- **Column function**: This function returns one or multiple columns of data. Take a look at the following code snippet:

```
//Syntax
column(StepName.selection, [ column1, column2, ..... )

//For example,
column(Static_Country_1.selection, [\"value\"])
returns all the country values.
[India, Japan, Brazil, China, ...]
```

- **Cell function**: This function returns a single value from the source data/step/result. Take a look at the following code snippet:

```
//Syntax
cell(StepName.selection), rowIndex, columnName)

//For example,
cell(Static_Country_1.selection), 0, [\"value\"]) returns 'India'.
```

- **Row function:** This function returns single-row data or multiple-row data. Take a look at the following code snippet:

```
//Syntax
 row(StepName.selection), [rowIndices...], [column1,
 column2, .... ])

//For example,
 row(Static_Country_1.selection), [0, 1, 2], [\"value\" ])
 returns 'India', 'Japan'
```

Let's take a look at the following diagram depicting the preceding functions:

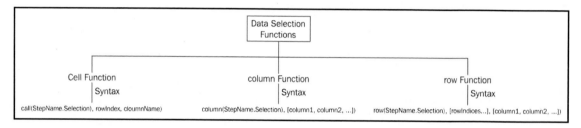

Data serialization functions

The functions in the following table convert data into a form consumable by a step where it is inserted:

Function name	Brief	Syntax	Example	Result
asDateRange()	Returns the date range filter condition as a string for a SAQL query.			
asEquality()	Returns an equality or in filter condition as a string for a SAQL query.			

`asGrouping()`	Returns a grouping as a string for a SAQL query.			
`asObject()`	Passes data without serialization.	`inputData.asObject()`	`column(Static_Country_1.selection, [\"value\"]).asObject()`	Selected country [India].
`asOrder()`	Returns the sort order as a string for a SAQL query.			
`asProjection()`	Returns the query expression and alias as a string.			
`asRange()`	Returns a range filter condition as a string for a SAQL query.			
`asString()`	Returns the string.	`inputdata.asString()`		

Now that we are familiar with binding functions, let's bind static steps and KPI steps by performing the following steps:

1. Open `Executive Dashboard for Sale` in edit mode and select the KPI widget for `Actual Closed_Won_1`.
2. Check the step name for that widget:

3. Press *Ctrl + E*. This will open the dashboard in JSON mode.
4. Search for your step in JSON by using *Ctrl + F* and go to the filtering label:

```
"filters": [
    [
        "IsClosed",
        [
            "true"
        ],
        "in"
    ]
]
},
```

5. As shown in the following code snippet, add the highlighted code snippet to filters:

```
"filters": [
    [
    "IsClosed",
        [
            "true"
        ],
          "in"
    ],
    [
    "Account.BillingCountry",
    "{{column(Static_Country_1.selection,
[\"value\"]).asObject()}}"
    ]
]
```

6. Click on **Done** and preview the dashboard.
7. Select the country from country list and observe that `Actual Amount won` is changing after selecting a country.

8. Repeat the same steps for the second widget:

Result binding

In result binding, the result of one step is used to calculate another step. This type of binding is used to create complex steps. This binding is only available in Wave Dashboard Designer.

As examples, we will do the following things:

1. Changing color dynamically depending upon value
2. Addition and multiplication of two steps

Let's create a new step that will be calculated from the result of `Actual_Closed_Won_Pr_1` minus `Actual_Closed_Won_1`. We'll get this by using result binding. Let's perform the following steps:

1. Add a third Number widget and click on the button in it to create a new step.
2. Create a new step and name it `Current_vs_Prior_Comparision`.
3. Change the mode to SAQL Mode and click on **Done**.

4. Select the widget and find the step name:

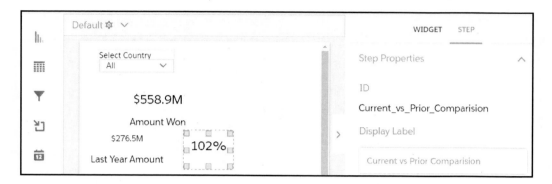

5. Press *Ctrl + E* to go to JSON mode and search for the step name
   `Current_vs_Prior_Comparision`:

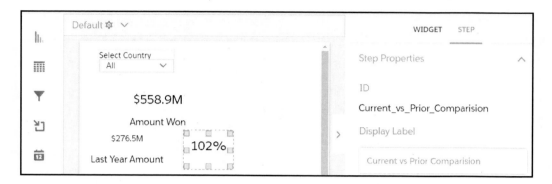

```
274        },
275 ▾    "Current_vs_Prior_Comparision": {
276          "broadcastFacet": true,
277          "groups": [],
278          "numbers": [],
279          "query": "q = load \"opportunities\";\nq = group q by all;\nq = foreach q generate (({{coalesce(column
               (Actual_Closed_Won_1.result,[\"sum_Amount\"]),0).asObject()}} - {{coalesce(column(Actual_Closed_Won_Pr_1
               .result,[\"sum_Amount\"]),0).asObject()}})/{{coalesce(column(Actual_Closed_Won_Pr_1.result
               ,[\"sum_Amount\"]),0).asObject()}})*100 as 'sum_percent'; \nq = limit q 2000;",
280          "receiveFacet": true,
281          "selectMode": "single",
282          "strings": [],
283          "type": "saql",
284          "useGlobal": true,
285 ▾        "visualizationParameters": {
286 ▾          "parameters": {
287              "autoFitMode": "none",
288              "showValues": true,
```

6. Search for the label `"query  :"` and replace it with the following code snippet:

```
"query": "q = load \"opportunities\";\nq = group q by all;\nq =
foreach q generate
(({{coalesce(column(Actual_Closed_Won_1.result,[\"sum_Amount\"]),0)
.asObject()}} -
{{coalesce(column(Actual_Closed_Won_Pr_1.result,[\"sum_Amount\"]),0
).asObject()}})/{{coalesce(column(Actual_Closed_Won_Pr_1.result,[\"
sum_Amount\"]),0).asObject()}})*100 as 'sum_percent'; \nq = limit q
2000;",
```

7. Click on **Done**. You should see the percentage value now.
8. Save the dashboard:

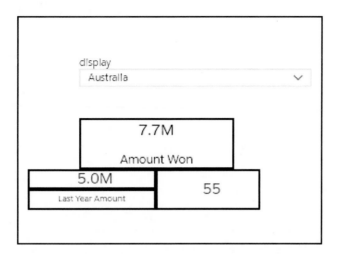

Formatting derived measures or fields

Our KPIs look great now, but they are still missing some formatting. We need to add the $ symbol to the first and second widgets and % to the third widget. There are the following two ways to make this change:

1. Make changes in the XMD file
2. Use the Wave lab tool by Heroku

To understand formatting fields by modifying XMD, refer to this link: `https://developer.salesforce.com/docs/atlas.enus.bi_dev_guide_xmd.meta/bi_dev_guide_xmd/`.

We are going to use the Wave lab tool for formatting. This tool uses an easy, point and click method to add formatting to fields. Let's perform the following steps:

1. Go to this link: `https://wave-labs.herokuapp.com/tools.html`.
2. Select **Production** and then log in.

3. Click on **XMD Editor** as shown in the following screenshot:

The XMD editor will open in a new tab.

4. Click on the **Open** button and select your dataset, as shown in the following screenshot:

5. Click on **Derived Measures** from the left panel and click on the **Derived Measures** button.

6. Fill in all the fields as shown in the following screenshot:

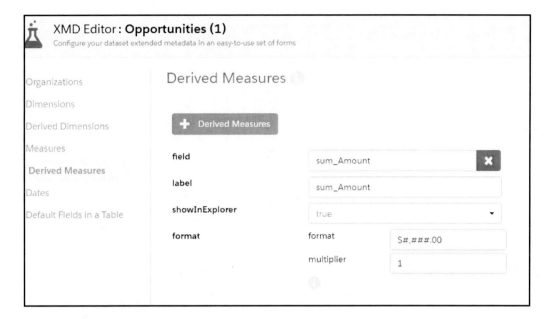

7. Click on the Save icon:

8. Now go to your dashboard and refresh it. You should see formatting as shown in the following screenshot:

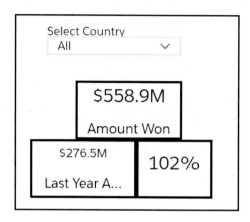

Funnel charts for Opportunities by Stage

Funnel charts are the best way to compress a huge amount of information and display the progress in a compact form. Funnel is the most useful chart when it comes to displaying deal flow and progress. It is a very important chart in sales or executive dashboards. So, let's create a Funnel chart to display open opportunities in different stages. We'll also connect it with our Static_Country list and owner list.

1. Create a new step and name it StageFunnel
2. Add **Sum** as **Measures** for the **Amount** field
3. Under **Group by**, select **Stage**, and under **Filter by** set **Closed Equals** as false
4. Click on **Add**
5. Change the chart type to **Funnel** and click on **Done**
6. Drag and drop the step into the dashboard

Now let's create two lists, for owners and account type, by performing the following steps:

1. Drag and drop the list widget onto the dashboard
2. Click on the middle button on the list and select the **Opportunity** dataset (if it is not selected automatically)
3. Search for the **Owner.Name** field and click on **Create**

This will create a list of all owners. Repeat the same steps for a second list widget and add the **Account.Type** field to create the list. Remember that we are using only one dataset, so these list widgets will automatically filter and update the dashboard upon value selection:

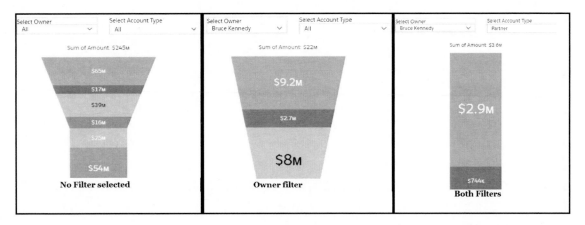

You can also see that the Funnel chart is not responding to the `Static_Country` list. This is because the `Static_Country` list is not part of the same dataset. Faceting won't connect it via a funnel. So, let's connect the Funnel chart to the static step. To do so, we need to add a filter using the column function. Open your dashboard in edit mode and press *Ctrl + E* to open JSON. Add the following highlighted code in the filter label for the Funnel chart step:

```
"filters": [
[
"IsClosed",
[
"false"
],
"in"
],
[
"Account.BillingCountry",
"{{column(Static_Country_1.selection, [\"value\"]).asObject()}}"
]
]
```

Take a look at the following screenshot:

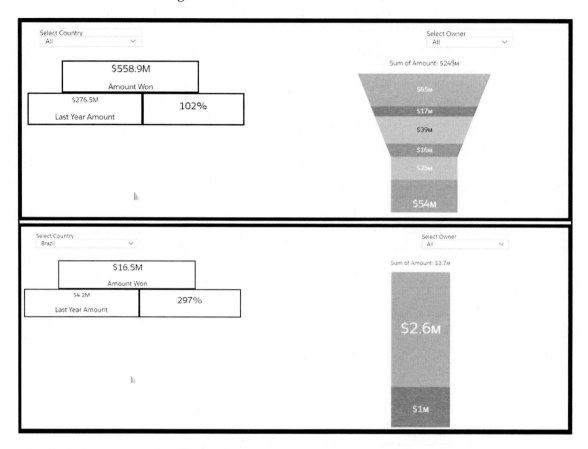

Now, let's create a table to show the number of closed opportunities and amount this month by owner. A table is a very important visualization tool for displaying record-level details on the dashboard. We can also apply sorting to the columns to get the highest and lowest record details for the dashboard. Follow these steps to create the table:

1. Drag and drop the Table widget from widget list
2. Click on the middle button, ▦ Table
3. Switch to Table Mode and select **Values Table**
4. Add and remove columns as required
5. Click on **Done**
6. Use table properties to fine-tune it

7. You can use the default themes provided by Einstein
8. Add coloring to the rows as shown in the following screenshot:

#	Account.BillingCountry	Account.Industry	Account.AccountSource	Account Annual Revenue	Account.Name	Account.Type
1	Canada	Finance	Employee Referral	500,000	Duncan535 Inc	Partner
2	Belgium	Banking	Trade Show	2,000,000	Bowers460 Inc	Partner
3	Singapore	Apparel	Advertisement	2,000,000	Collins928 Inc	Customer
4	Hong Kong	Insurance	Advertisement	2,000,000	Holmes945 Inc	Customer
5	Spain	Insurance	Partner	700,000,000	Jefferson853 Inc	Customer
6	USA	Banking	Web	700,000	Sharp908 Inc	Customer
7	USA	Technology	Employee Referral	2,000,000	Oliver959 Inc	Partner
8	Canada	Energy	Employee Referral	700,000	Ross559 Inc	Partner

Sales Cloud Einstein

Sales Cloud for Einstein is a tool that is provided to increase the productivity of your sales team. It includes key features such as **Lead Scoring**, **Opportunity Insights**, and so on. Sales Cloud Einstein is a complete AI solution for sales teams and increases sales productivity with machine learning and business sentiment analysis. This is a purchased feature. After you purchase Sales Cloud Einstein, Salesforce installs two packages in your organization, `SalesforceIQ` Cloud, and `Sales Insights`. Each package adds an associated integration user and profile. Salesforce uses these entities to provide insights into your organization. If you update these entities, it can affect your organization's ability to get insights.

Sales Cloud Einstein is only available to users with standard Salesforce licenses.

For Lead Scoring

Atleast 1,000 leads must have been created over the last six months in your Salesforce organization.

Setting up Sales Cloud Einstein

Here are the steps you'll need to follow to set up your Sales Cloud Einstein:

Creating a permission set

Create a permission set with the Sales Cloud Einstein permission set license from **Setup** by performing the following steps:

1. Enter `Permission Sets` in the **Quick Find / Search...** box
2. Select **Permission Sets** under **Manage Users**
3. Click on **New** and enter a name for the permission set
4. Name it `Einstein for Sale`
5. From the **License** drop-down list, select **Sales Cloud Einstein**
6. Click on **Save** and click on **App Permissions**
7. Click on **Edit** and enable application permissions for Einstein features
8. Click on **Save**

Assigning permission sets to users

Let's take a look at the following steps to assign Einstein licenses to users from **Setup**:

1. Enter `Users` in the **Quick Find / Search...** box, then select **Users**
2. Select a user
3. In the **Permission Set Assignments** related list, click on **Edit Assignments**
4. Add the **Sales Cloud Einstein** permission set under **Enabled Permission Sets** and click **Save**
5. Repeat the process for the other users you want to grant access to

The number of permission sets you can assign is limited by the number of feature licenses you've purchased. The following are the key features of Sales Cloud Einstein:

- Einstein Activity Capture for Sales Cloud Einstein
- Einstein Lead Scoring
- Einstein Opportunity Insights
- Einstein Account Insights
- Einstein Automated Contacts

The Sales Analytics Apps license

The Sales Analytics Apps license unlocks the power of Sales Cloud for sales teams. This is an in-built application that provides insights to managers, executives, representatives, and so on. The Sales Analytics home dashboard tells you about closed deals, win rate, average deal amount, and average days in a sales cycle. It also gives you information about your goals in one glance, as shown in the following screenshot:

This application includes the following feature dashboards:

- Leaderboard
- Trending
- Forecast
- Activities
- An overview of dashboards for executives, sales representatives, and sales stages
- Team benchmark and team whitespace

Creating a Sales Analytics App

Creating Sales Analytics Apps is pretty easy. Switch back to Salesforce Classic, go to **Permission Sets,** and create one by performing the following steps:

1. Create a permission set named `The Sales Analytics App`
2. Select the **Sales Analytics Apps** permission set license
3. Assign a permission set to an individual user

Now that you have assigned the permission set to your user, switch back to **Analytics Studio** again:

1. Navigate to **Analytics Studio | Create | App**
2. Select **Sales Analytics** and click on **Continue**
3. Click on **Looks good, next**
4. Select **Basic** and click on **Looks good, next**
5. Name your application `Basic Sales Analytics app`
6. Click on **Create**

When Salesforce is done creating the application, you will get a notification email.

Refresh the page after you receive the email. You can see all the dashboards, lenses, and datasets that have been created.

For rapid application creation, choose **Basic** creation as it uses the default settings. The Sales Analytics App creation process does not support Internet Explorer 11, but users can view the application after it has been created. The Sales Analytics App license is a single-user license that provides access to Sales Analytics.

To check all the dashboards and lenses related to this application, navigate to **Analytics Studio | App | Sales Analytics,** as shown in the following screenshot:

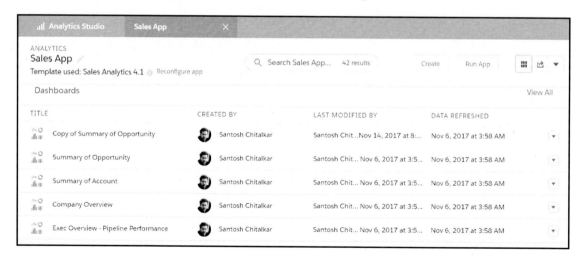

Summary

In this chapter, we saw that the executive dashboard provides very important business insights about data. We also learned how to connect components on the dashboard by using bindings and the binding functions provided by Einstein. We also saw how to use result binding to create steps that are based upon the results of another step. This binding is used to built complex steps. Einstein Analytics provides sales analytics in order to increase the productivity of sales teams.

We also learned how we can utilize the built-in dashboards to create sales applications, how to format fields by modifying the XMD file, and how to use the Wave lab application, Heroku.

In the next chapter, we will see when and where to use data manipulation functions. We are also going to learn about custom settings and their uses. We will also cover Service Cloud Einstein and Lead Score.

6
Einstein at Your Service

Sales Cloud Einstein provides sales forecasting and predictive analysis for data. Companies that are into sales spend huge amounts of time and effort on sales forecasting and prediction. Sales Cloud Einstein predictions are more accurate and hence increase the productivity of sales teams. It is very important for a business to satisfy their customers to earn their loyalty. A great service experience impresses the customer, and with Service Cloud Einstein we can achieve this. This chapter is completely practical. In this chapter, we are going to cover the following topics:

- Building a complete dashboard for services
- Connecting static steps to dashboard components
- Dashboard Inspector
- Einstein custom actions

Service dashboards

The executive board of Anutosh Infotech spends a lot of time checking customer satisfaction. They want to build a dashboard that can give them an easy way to understand customer services and help them improve their customer relationships. They want the following information on the dashboard:

- Number of open cases by country in the current year
- KPI for total open cases, closed cases, and total cases in the current year
- Count of cases closed every month by account sources
- Filter option to control lenses on the dashboard

Customer service dashboard – VP

We are going to create a customer service dashboard. Let's set up a dashboard layout first, with the following widgets:

- Add four **List** widgets horizontally
- One **Toggle** widget
- Three **Number** widgets for KPI
- Two **Chart** widgets
- Three **Text** widgets

Adjust the layout, as shown in the following screenshot:

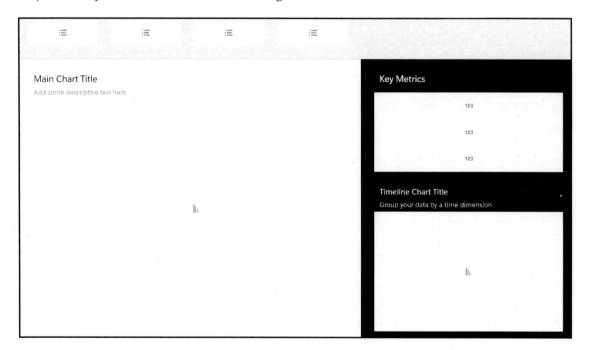

Dashboards and lenses

Now that we have set the template for the dashboard, let's create the steps/lenses for the widgets.

Creating list filters

A List widget is a filter widget that gives the user the flexibility to add filters to dashboard data. Let's create a List widget by performing the following steps:

1. Go to the **List** widget and click on the ☰ button in the middle.
2. Check which dataset is selected. It should be a the **Cases** dataset. If it is not the **Cases** dataset, then select it by using the **Change Dataset** option:

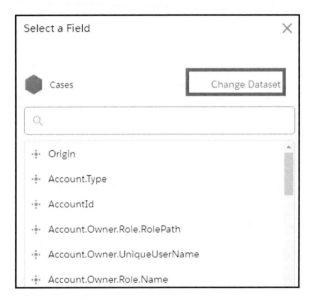

3. Select the **Account.Type** field.
4. Click on the **Create** button.
5. Repeat the preceding steps for the other three list widgets and select the **Account.Industry**, **Account.Owner.Role.Name**, and **Status** fields. Your dashboard will look like the following screenshot:

Static steps for country

Let's perform the following steps to create a static step for country:

1. Click anywhere on the dashboard, except widgets, and you should see the **Create Step** button on the right-hand side panel.
2. Click on the **Create Step** button, then click on **Create a Static Step with Custom Values**.
3. Enter `Static_Country` in the **Display Label** field.
4. Enter the country name `India` in the **DISPLAY** and **VALUE** labels and click on **Add**.
5. Repeat this by adding different country names, as shown in the following screenshot:

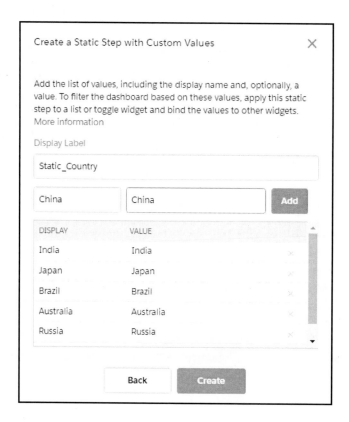

6. After adding all required country values, click on **Create**. You can see the static step in the **STEP** panel now. Go to JSON mode by pressing *Ctrl + E*. Your complete `Static_Country` code is as follows:

```
"Static_Country_1": {
                    "type": "staticflex",
                    "start": {
                        "display": [
                            "India"
                        ]
                    },
                    "values": [
                        {
                            "display": "India",
                            "value": "India"
                        },
                        {
                            "display": "China",
                            "value": "China"
                        },
                        {
                            "display": "Canada",
                            "value": "Canada"
                        },
                        {
                            "display": "USA",
                            "value": "USA"
                        },
                        {
                            "display": "Japan",
                            "value": "Japan"
                        },
                        {
                            "display": "Australia",
                            "value": "Australia"
                        },
                        {
                            "display": "Germany",
                            "value": "Germany"
                        },
                        {
                            "display": "Russian",
                            "value": "Russian"
                        },
                        {
                            "display": "Brazil",
                            "value": "Brazil"
```

```
                                 }
                               ],
                               "useGlobal": false,
                               "isGlobal": false,
                               "selectMode": "single",
                               "label": "Static_Country"
                             },
```

Map chart for BillingCountry

A map chart expands the analytic visualization capabilities. We can display the data related to the same geographical component together on a world map or in an individual country. We can use this map chart in both the Classic as well as Wave Designer dashboards. Let's create a map chart to display the number of open cases by country by performing the following steps:

1. Click on **Create Step** and name it `Billing Country Map`.
2. Select the **Cases** dataset.
3. Add **Sum** as **Measures** and select the **Opportunity.Amount** field.
4. Select **Account.BillingCountry** under **Group by**.
5. Add a filter for **Closed Date, Less Than Or Equal To** for the current year and **Closed, Equals** and **Open**. Click on **Add**.
6. Click on **Done**.
7. Add a Chart widget to the dashboard and drag and drop the `Billing Country Map` step onto the widget.
8. Change the **Bar** chart to a **Map** by using chart settings:

Maps are not case-sensitive, but entities such as US states and world countries are exceptions, and they should be entered in the same manner.

Fine-tuning maps using map properties

We can fine-tune the map by using the properties. We can configure the maps to autozoom on a selected area. We can also set the value range to high, medium, and low to highlight countries in color, as shown in the following screenshot:

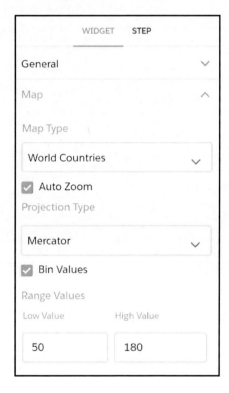

Let's change the map theme to **Dark** from the **General** section. Now, expand the **Map** section and select the **Auto Zoom** checkbox and **Bin Values**. As we are displaying the row counts for cases from every country, let's add some color coding so that the user can understand the number of cases raised per country with just one look. Set the bin values for this, as shown in the following screenshot:

The BillingCountry and BillingState tables

Tables show detailed information on the dashboard. In Einstein, we can build value, pivot, and compare tables. Compare Tables can be used to define columns with formulas. Let's take a look at the following steps:

1. Click on **Create Step** on the right-hand side, and name it as `Billing Country Table`
2. Add **Sum** as **Measures** and select the **Opportunity.Amount** field
3. Select **Account.BillingCountry** under **Group by** and then group it by **Account.BillingState**
4. Switch to Table Mode and select **Compare Table**

5. Add a filter for the **Close Date, Less Than Or Equal To** for the current year
6. Click on **Done**
7. Add a Table widget to the dashboard and drag and drop `Billing Country Table` onto the widget

Connecting static steps as filters to the map and table

Now that we have the country static step, map chart, and table in place, let's connect them to each other so that when a user clicks on the country toggle, both table and map chart respond. We will do this by performing the following steps:

1. Open your dashboard and press *Ctrl + E*
2. In JSON mode, search for the map step, which is `Account_BillingCountry`, and look for a filter label
3. Add the following code:

```
[ "Account.BillingCountry",
 "{{column(Static_Country_1.selection, [\"value\"]).asObject()}}",
 "in"
 ],
```

Adding key matrics to the dashboard using a Number widget

KPI shows important information about the business. Number widgets are very important for creating KPIs. For our dashboard, we need to create three KPIs for open, closed, and total number of cases. Let's create KPIs by performing the following steps:

1. Click on the **Create Step** button and name it as `Open Case`; select the **Cases** dataset.
2. Select **Measures** as **Sum** and select the **Opportunity.Amount** field.
3. Select the **Filter by** field as **Closed, Equals**, and then select **Open**. Click on **Add**.
4. Again, under the **Filter by** option, select **Closed Date** and click on the **Relative to now** option. Click on **Years** and select the current year.
5. Click on **Add** and then click on **Done**.

6. Drag and drop it onto the step on the **Number** widget and fine-tune it. Clone the same step and change the filter for the **Closed** field to **Close** and clone it one more time. Remove the **Closed** filter field:

The Timeline chart for case count by AccountSources

The Timeline chart is used to display the changes in value over time. It is a line chart, and at least one axis of this chart must have a time dimension. Let's use this chart to display the count of closed cases by **AccountSources** overtime. As per our client's requirement, we need to show a month to month timeline. Let's perform the following steps:

1. Click on the button in the middle of the Chart widget for the **Timeline** chart, and select a **Cases** dataset
2. Group it by **Closed Date**; grouping should be done by **Months**
3. Add one more grouping for the **Account.AccountSources** field
4. Under **Filter by** add a filter for **Closed**, **Equals** as **True/Open filter** field
5. Change Chart Mode to **Timeline** chart, as shown in the following screenshot:

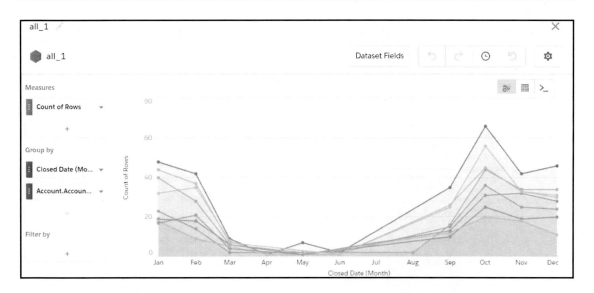

6. Click on **Done**

Broadcast faceting

As we have already gone through the facet feature in the last chapters, we know that faceting is the easiest and simplest way to connect components on a dashboard. All the components of the same dataset can communicate with each other via faceting. By default, faceting is enabled for components of the same dataset. Now, what is **broadcast faceting**? How it is related to the **Facet** option and where can we use it? Consider a use case where you have created multiple visualizations for the **Opportunity** dataset and the client says, "When I select one particular visualization, I don't want others to filter data." This is when we can use the broadcasting facet feature.

A broadcasting facet decides whether or not to apply faceting/filters to other components on the dashboard. You can find this option in the **STEP** tab as shown in the following screenshot:

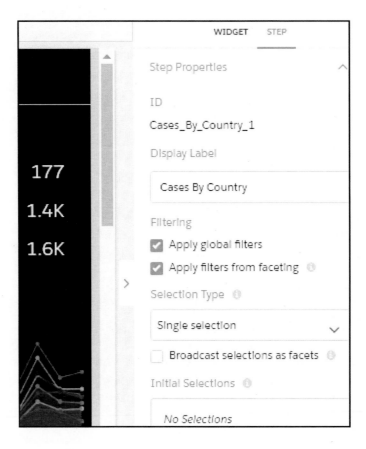

So let's apply this to our `Customer Service Dashboard - VP` dashboard. Open the dashboard in edit mode and select the map chart. In the step property panel, click on the **STEP** tab and deselect **Broadcast selections as facets**. Now preview the dashboard and select any country. Observe that other components are not affected/filtered, as shown in the following screenshot:

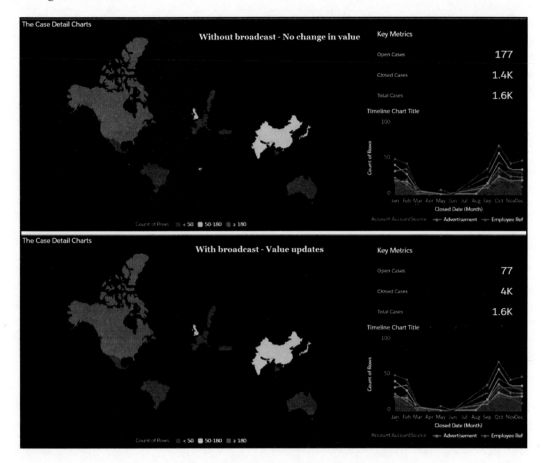

Observe that the Key Metrics in without broadcast do not change and the same parameters change for with broadcast

Disable the **Broadcast selections as facets** option when you do not want to filter other faceted components upon selection of a particular chart. The **Broadcast selections as facets** option appear as read-only for the aggregate, grain, and static step types. It appears as read-only for SAQL steps also, as these steps do not support faceting.

Optimizing dashboard performance

Optimization is very important to get the best out of a design, and it maximizes the performance of the dashboard. Optimization includes factors such as reliability and efficiency. Einstein provides a feature called **Dashboard Inspector**, which runs a performance check on the dashboard and ensures that everything runs optimally. If we built a complex dashboard with SAQL, selection binding, result binding, and by changing JSON, then it is important to run a performance check to ensure all steps runs properly. The **Dashboard Inspector** feature identifies issues in steps and queries, and recommends performance improvements. So let's run the dashboard inspector for our dashboard by performing the following steps, and let's see what result we get:

1. Open the dashboard in preview mode and click on the three dots, as shown in the following screenshot:

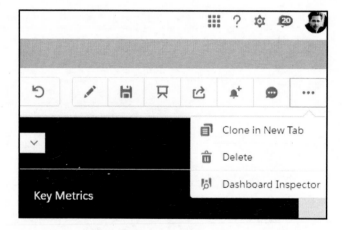

 Remember that **Dashboard Inspector** is not available while running the application.

2. Click on **Dashboard Inspector**.

3. Click on the **PERFORMANCE** tab to run the performance check, as shown in the following screenshot:

4. Click on the **Run Performance Check** button and wait for the result, as shown in the following screenshot:

4. Now you can see the factors affecting the performance of the dashboard. Remove unused steps and optimize queries. After changing all necessary performance factors, run the dashboard inspector again.

 If you have multiple layouts for a single dashboard then you need to run performance checks for each layout separately. The **Dashboard Inspector** feature gives the results only for the current page, not for all the dashboards in an organization.

Einstein custom actions

Einstein custom actions enable a user to perform tasks such as creating records and updating records. Einstein custom actions are reusable across platforms. These are built on dashboards and hence save a lot of time and increase productivity. Einstein custom actions are available on Sales Cloud, Service Cloud, and Analytics Cloud, as shown in the following diagram:

Sales cloud   Service cloud   Analytics Cloud

 The availability of custom actions is completely dependent on the permissions and the application sharing access given to the user.

What is a Salesforce action?

Using actions, a user can perform actions such as opening records and updating records from Einstein Analytics without exiting from it. These actions can be added in two places, such as charts and tables. Actions allow Einstein Analytics to directly interact with Salesforce records. Using these actions, a user can quickly execute common tasks such as opening records, updating, Chatter post, and so on, from the dashboard. A user can also use quick actions created on Salesforce objects.

Use dimensions to add an action menu. Einstein allows us to create actions on dimensions, not measures. Users can only see actions that are assigned to page layouts.

Let's create an action that will open a related opportunity record in URL. So, without further ado, let's perform the following steps:

1. Go to **Analytics Studio | DATASETS**.
2. Select **Opportunities**, or any dataset, as shown in the following screenshot:

3. A dataset will open in edit mode. Click on **Configure Actions**:

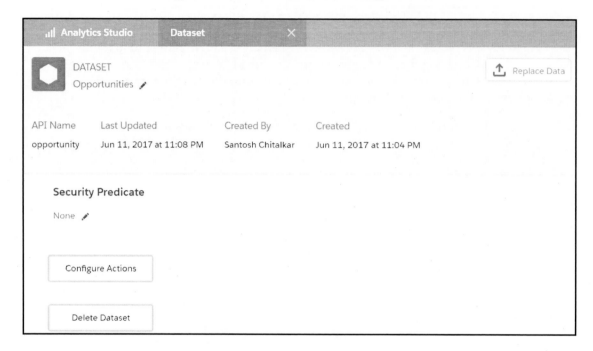

4. After clicking on **Configure Actions**, a popup will open, showing all fields in the dataset, as shown in the following screenshot:

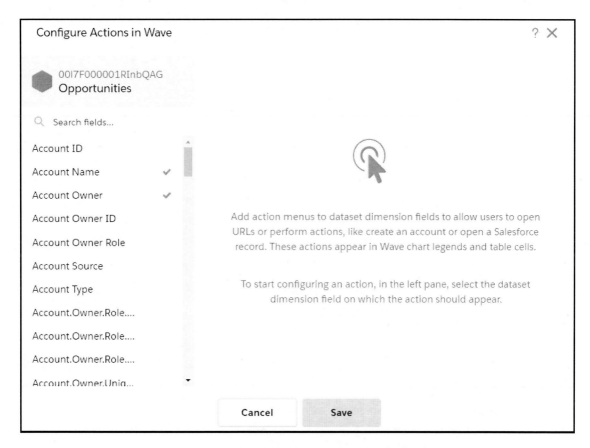

5. Search for the **Opportunity ID** field or the name field.
6. Now scroll down and click on **Perform Salesforce actions**.

7. Now select the **Choose actions** option. You can either select one or you can select all, as shown in the following screenshot:

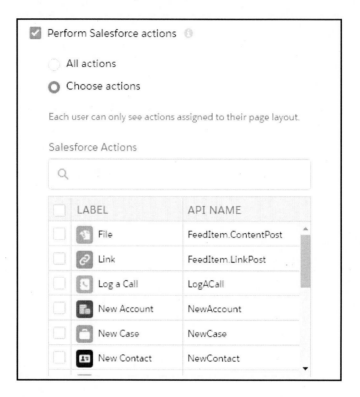

8. Click on **Save**.
9. Now open any dashboard and create an opportunity table with the Opportunity ID, Account Name, and Account ID field columns.
10. Go to preview mode and hover over the record; you will see a downward arrow.

11. Click on it and you should see all selected actions, as shown in the following screenshot:

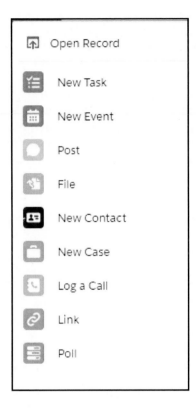

Custom actions defined in Salesforce are accessible from Einstein's custom action menu. You can post to Chatter, create an event or opportunity, or update a record and go directly to Salesforce records.

 Actions on contacts, users, or user profile page layouts are not supported. Actions are reusable across platforms, including Mobile and Einstein Analytics. The current implementation of action menus supports Chatter actions (**Post**, **File**, **Link**, and **Poll**).

Summary

Now that we have finished with this chapter, we know that **List** widgets are filter widgets. We also looked at how custom actions can be performed and how broadcasting helps dashboard components communicate. We also covered how the dashboard increases productivity.

Creating datasets has been made easier by Einstein. But so many times it happens that we use so many fields unnecessarily in a dataset, or we might forget a file in the data. How do we tackle such problems? We can use a feature called **Recipe**, which we are going to study in the next chapter; this chapter also includes data preparation, data recipes, scheduling recipes, and exporting datasets from Einstein using `datasetUtils`.

7
Security and Sharing in Einstein Analytics

Data security is the most important aspect of any business, irrespective of the size of the business. The platform security should be able to protect sensitive and confidential data. Protecting data from any unauthorized user is very important and Einstein Analytics Security ensures that. It makes sure that the right users have the right to access to the right data. As you already know, there are two main sources from which we import data into Einstein and build datasets, Salesforce data, and external systems. The **Einstein Analytics Security** model provides multiple ways to secure this data. This chapter covers security and sharing in Einstein Analytics. In this chapter, we are going to cover the following topics:

- Salesforce data access
- Configuring integration/security users
- Sharing applications, lenses, and dashboards
- Data security, security predicates, and sharing inheritance
- Implementing row-level security

Einstein Security

Before starting on security in Einstein Analytics, it is important to set up your organization, defining user types so that it is available to use. We have already covered this topic in Chapter 2, *Setting Up Einstein Analytics* under the *User types* section. Protecting data from breaches, theft, or from any unauthorized user is very important. The following are some key points of data security in Einstein:

- Salesforce admins can restrict access to data by setting up field-level security and object-level security in Salesforce. These settings prevent data flow from loading sensitive Salesforce data into a dataset.
- Dataset owners can restrict data access by using row-level security.
- Analytics supports security predicates, a robust row-level security feature that enables you to model many different types of access control on datasets.
- Analytics also supports sharing inheritance.

 To implement sharing inheritance, security predicates are mandatory.

Take a look at the following diagram:

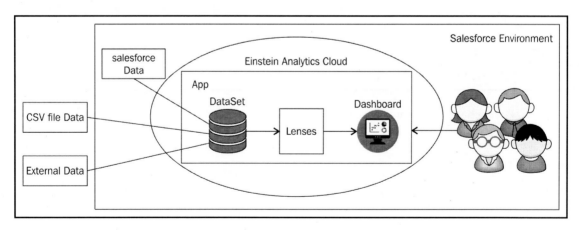

Salesforce data security

In Einstein Analytics, dataflows bring the data to the Analytics Cloud from Salesforce. It is important that Einstein Analytics has all the necessary permissions and access to objects as well as fields. If an object or a field is not accessible to Einstein then the dataflow fails and it cannot extract data from Salesforce. So we need to make sure that the required access is given to the integration user and security user. We can configure the permission set for these users. Let's configure permissions for an integration user by performing the following steps:

1. Switch to classic mode and enter `Profiles` in the **Quick Find / Search...** box
2. Select and clone the **Analytics Cloud Integration User** profile and **Analytics Cloud Security User** profile for the integration user and security user respectively:

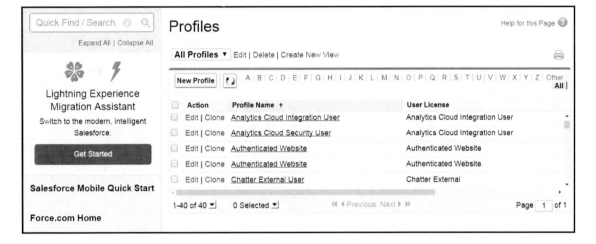

3. Save the cloned profiles and then edit them
4. Set the permission to **Read** for all objects and fields
5. Save the profile and assign it to users

> The best practice for configuring permissions for integration users and security users is to clone existing permissions and make changes in the cloned permission set.

Take a look at the following diagram:

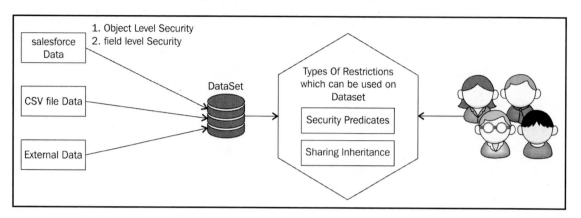

Data pulled from Salesforce can be made secure from both sides: Salesforce as well as Einstein Analytics. It is important to understand that Salesforce and Einstein Analytics are two independent databases. So, a user security setting given to Einstein will not affect the data in Salesforce. There are the following ways to secure data pulled from Salesforce:

Salesforce Security	Einstein Analytics Security
Roles and profiles	Inheritance security
Organization-Wide Defaults (OWD) and record ownership	Security predicates
Sharing rules	Application-level security

Sharing mechanism in Einstein

All Analytics users start off with **Viewer** access to the default **Shared App** that's available out-of-the-box; administrators can change this default setting to restrict or extend access. All other applications created by individual users are private, by default; the application owner and administrators have **Manager** access and can extend access to other Users, groups, or roles. The following diagram shows how the sharing mechanism works in Einstein Analytics:

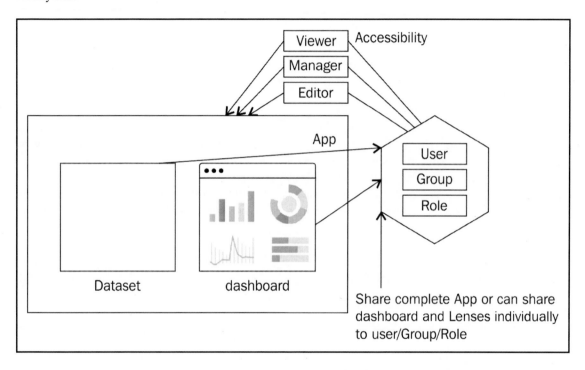

Here's a summary of what users can do with **Viewer**, **Editor**, and **Manager** access:

Action / Access level	Viewer	Editor	Manager
View dashboards, lenses, and datasets in the application. If the underlying dataset is in a different application than a lens or dashboard, the user must have access to both applications to view the lens or dashboard.	Yes	Yes	Yes
See who has access to the application.	Yes	Yes	Yes

Save contents of the application to another application that the user has **Editor** or **Manager** access to.	Yes	Yes	Yes
Save changes to existing dashboards, lenses, and datasets in the application (saving dashboards requires the appropriate permission set license and permission).		Yes	Yes
Change the application's sharing settings.			Yes
Rename the application.			Yes
Delete the application.			Yes

 The Salesforce database and Einstein Analytics database are both different, so security for them is also separate.

Confidentiality, integrity, and availability together are referred to as the CIA Triad and it is designed to help organizations decide what security policies to implement within the organization. Salesforce knows that keeping information private and restricting access by unauthorized users is essential for business. By sharing the application, we can share a lens, dashboard, and dataset all together with one click. To share the entire application, do the following:

1. Go to your Einstein Analytics and then to **Analytics Studio**
2. Click on the **APPS** tab and then the icon for your application that you want to share, as shown in the following screenshot:

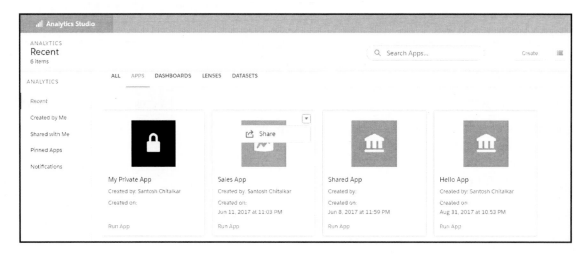

3. Click on **Share** and it will open a new popup window, as shown in the following screenshot:

Using this window, you can share the application with an individual user, a group of users, or a particular role

4. You can define the access level as **Viewer**, **Editor**, or **Manager**
5. After selecting **User**, click on the user you wish to add and click on **Add**
6. Save and then close the popup

And that's it. It's done.

Mass-sharing the application

Sometimes, we are required to share the application with a wide audience:

1. There are multiple approaches to mass-sharing the Wave application such as by role or by username
2. In Salesforce classic UI, navigate to **Setup**|**Public Groups** | **New**
3. For example, to share a sales application, label a public group as `Analytics_Sales_Group`

4. Search and add users to a group by **Role**, **Roles and Subordinates**, or by **Users** (username):

5. In Wave, go to Sales App and open **GIVE ACCESS** as shown in the following screenshot:

6. Search for the `Analytics_Sales` public group
7. Add the **Viewer** option as shown in the following screenshot:

8. Click on **Save**

Row-level security

Access to a dataset means access to all records in a dataset. Let's consider that xyz user has access to a dataset and within that dataset we have records, which have crucial and sensitive data. Giving access to this data means compromising security, which should not happen.

So in this case, to protect the sensitive data, we can use row-level security. We can add security predicates to each dataset that filter the data again and only give access to the records which we want. So what is this predicate?

A predicate is a filter condition that defines row-level access for each record from the dataset. Define a predicate for each dataset on which you want to restrict access to records. In other words, row-level security is enforced by a predicate.

The security predicate uses either a standard or custom field of user object and filters dataset records. It matches the fields with particular dimensions in your dataset. We can also use a combination of multiple predicates by using logical operators such as &, ||, and so on.

To add a security predicate perform the following steps:

1. Navigate to the **Analytics Studio** | **DATASETS** tab.
2. Click on the ▾ icon and click on **Edit** to edit the dataset as shown in the following screenshot:

3. Scroll down and you should see the **Security** section under which a user can add security predicates as shown in the following screenshot:

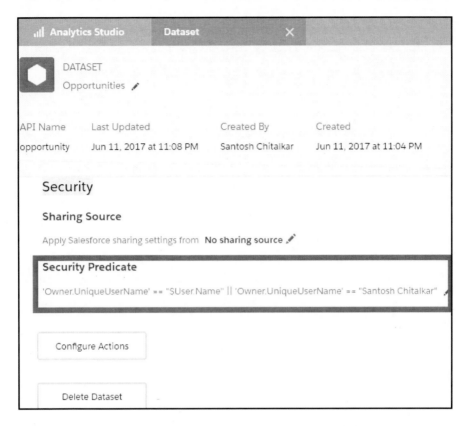

4. We can use this approach to filter out data from the dataset that is already uploaded to the platform. We can also apply security predicates before data is uploaded. If we are uploading any external datasets then we can add a security predicate using the `rowLevelSecurityFilter` node in the schema file:

```
//For example
"'OwnerId' == \"$User.Name\"").
```

Using escape characters is required.

 When using this option for implementation, make sure to log out and log back into the organization to see the security predicate take effect.

A user can also add security predicates while registering a dataset in the `rowLevelSecurityFilter` node. Here is the code snippet:

```
"Register_Dataset": {

        "action": "sfdcRegister",

        "parameters": {

                "alias": "Dataset_Name",

                "name": "Dataset_Name",

                "source":
        "105_Augment_OpportunityTeamMember_Opportunity",

                "rowLevelSecurityFilter": "'OwnerId' ==
        \"$User.Id\""

                }
        }
```

The security predicate can only use fields from the `User` object to add security filters in the dataset.

Security predicates for the record owner

In this section, we are going to implement security predicates on a dataset. Let's create one dashboard:

1. Navigate to **Analytics Studio** | **Create** | **Dashboard** and select a blank dashboard.
2. Drag and drop one Chart widget to it.
3. Click on the ⊪ Chart button in the middle and select the **Opportunity** dataset.
4. Change the **Measures** option to **Sum** and select the **Amount** field.

5. Group it by **Lead Source**.
6. Click on **Done**.
7. Save the dashboard in `Hello App`.
8. Name the dashboard `Security dashboard` as shown in the following screenshot:

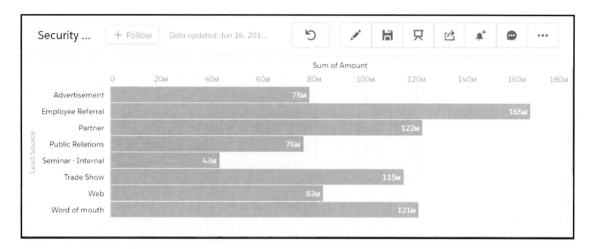

9. As this opportunity dataset does not have any security predicate applied to it, this dashboard will show all data/records to all the users. To verify this, exit from the Analytics platform and go to Salesforce Classic. Navigate to **Setup | Manage Users | Users** and log in as `Garza, Laura` as shown in the following screenshot:

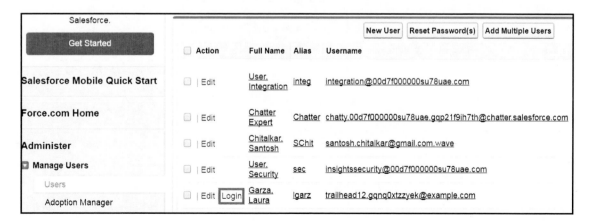

10. Now that you are logged in as `Garza Laura`, switch to Einstein Analytics and check for the `Security dashboard`, we created as shown in the following screenshot:

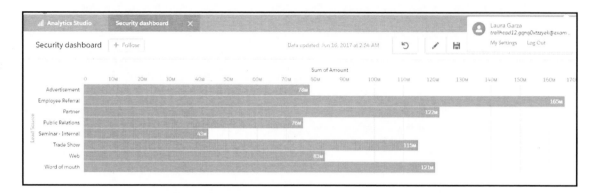

We can see that Laura can see all the records.

Now, let's log out from Laura and go to our previous user. Switch to Einstein Analytics and add a security predicate to the **Opportunity** dataset so that the user can only see those records that are owned by them. Let's perform the following steps:

1. Navigate to **Analytics Studio** and click on the **DATASETS** tab.
2. Click on the icon and click on **Edit** to edit the dataset as shown in the following screenshot:

3. Scroll down and you should see the **Security** section under which a user can add security predicates.

4. Add a **Security predicate** as `'OwnerId' == "$User.Id"`:

5. Now exit from the Analytics platform and follow the same steps explained earlier and log in as `Garza Laura`. Check the `Security dashboard`. You can see that the dashboard reflects only the data that is owned by Laura:

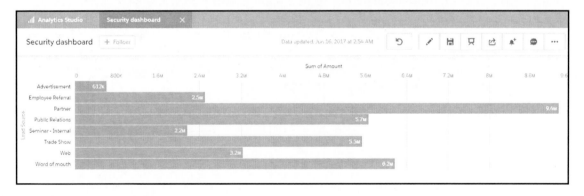

Observe how the value of all the bar charts in the preceding screenshot have changed after applying the User Id

This is the simplest implementation of a security predicate based on record ownership. There is no need to add any additional transformation to it. Simply compare `OwnerIds` and that is it.

In order to make this work, make sure that you are uploading an 18-digit `OwnerIds` and not a 15-digit one.

Record ownership security could be extended to team-based security. The implementation in this case would vary depending on the way that the object in question is structured.

Summary

Einstein Analytics provides the user with robust alternatives to control applications and data access for the platform. They can use Salesforce organization security to make sure that only predetermined data elements are imported into Einstein Analytics. Once the data is within Einstein, application-level security and the security predicate can be leveraged to implement different schemes, such as team-based security or management hierarchy-based security. Users can provide security to data from Salesforce by setting up a profile, and object-level and field-level security. Once the data is on the Einstein platform, the user can provide security to data with security predicates, which set row-level access. Einstein Analytics provides the option to share lenses, dashboards, and even entire applications with other users. A user can give **Viewer**, **Editor**, and **Manager** access to a shared component.

The Einstein Analytics platform knows that a business does not work on a single platform so dashboards and lenses have been made flexible enough to embed them with other platforms such as Lightning, Salesforce Classic, Community sites, and so on. In the next chapter, we are going to cover how we can embed a dashboard in a detail page in Salesforce Classic, Lightning, Visualforce Pages, and Community. We are also going to cover viewing analytics for communities, enabling analytics for communities, whitelisting trusted websites for embedded dashboards, and embedding dashboards in a record page and filtering them depending upon the record in Classic and Lightning.

8
Recipe in Einstein

While working with data, there are times where we realize that we have added a lot of unnecessary fields and data and we need to follow the process of removing them. We also need to add new fields to the same dataset where we have missed a required field or, in the future, if we need to add a new one. This is called data preparation and it is easier with Einstein Analytics. In this chapter, we are going to concentrate on the following topics:

- The dataset recipe
- Preparing data
- Combining two datasets and creating a new one
- The scheduling recipe
- Exporting datasets from Einstein using `datasetUtils`

Dataset recipe

So far we have created multiple datasets, such as opportunity, account, and quota. But we do not use all the fields in the dataset. So how do you remove them or what if I added a new field in Salesforce or to the external source of the dataset and I want to add that field to the dataset. We can use a data recipe user interface to do this. The data recipe provides the flexibility for the user to add required elements and to remove unnecessary elements. In the data recipe, you can map two datasets, side by side, and this results in a new dataset.

What is a data recipe?

A data recipe is a user interface tool that allows you to receive data from the existing datasets, replications, bucket fields, and so on, and prepare a new dataset from them. **Data Manager** is the place where you can find this tool. The interface of **Data Manager** is shown in the following screenshot:

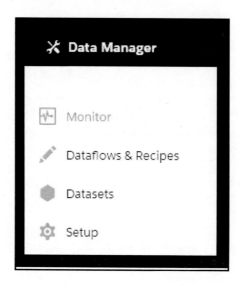

Creating a recipe

Using data recipes, we can combine data from different resources, such as different datasets, formula fields, bucket fields, replications, and we can also remove fields and rows that are not required to create a target dataset.

Let's take a look at the following diagram:

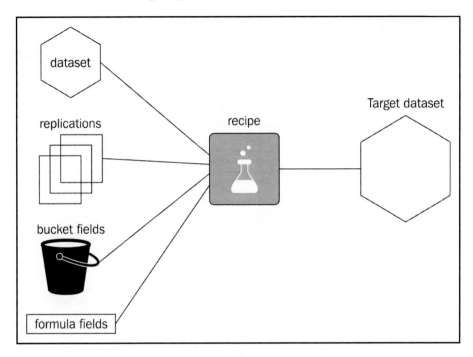

Let's create a dataset to display data from accounts and cases together:

1. To create a recipe, go to **Data Manager,** as shown in the following screenshot:

2. Click on **Dataflow & Recipes** and then select the **DATASET RECIPES** tab, as shown in the following screenshot:

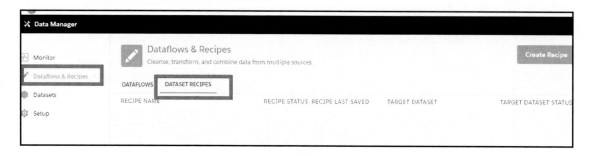

3. Click on the **Create Recipe** button at the right. It will open a window popup for selecting a base dataset for the recipe. This window gives the user the option to select either the **PUBLISHED** dataset or the **REPLICATED** dataset. The **REPLICATED** dataset tab appears when the user enables replications:

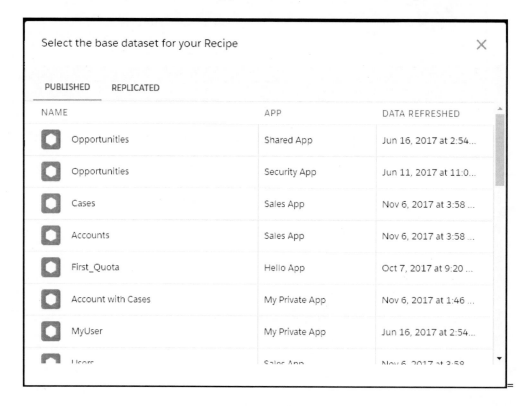

4. Select **Accounts** as the base dataset for the recipe and enter the name of your recipe, `Account_Cases`, and click on **Continue**:

Create a Recipe for This Dataset

Dataset Recipe Name

Cancel   Continue

 Remember that the recipe name will be used as the name for `Target Dataset`. You will also get the option to change the target dataset name before you create it.

5. After selecting the dataset, you can see the data in the table. Einstein Analytics provides a feature for previewing a recipe, where you can add or remove a number of fields and limit the number of rows displayed. This feature helps us to create a recipe faster if we are working on huge data:

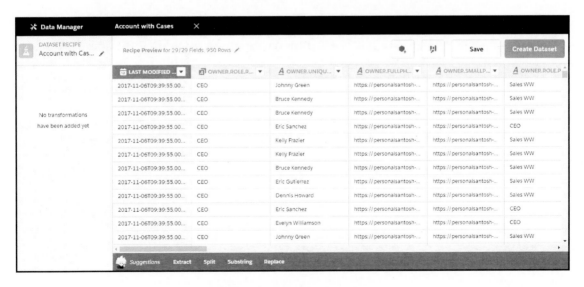

The preceding screenshot displays the recipe preview

6. Click on the **Add Data** button to add a second dataset and select the Cases dataset, which contains the lookup fields on which to base the dataset that is `Account`. After clicking on the second dataset, the next screen appears, where we can see and compare two datasets side by side, as shown in the following screenshot:

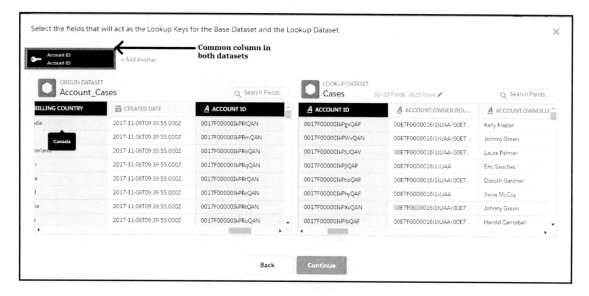

7. Einstein Analytics suggests a common column for merging two datasets. The user can also select a different merge key. To select or add different merge keys, click on the columns you wish to merge.
8. User can also add a key merge by clicking on **Add Another**.
9. Click on **Continue**.
10. On the next screen, the user can add/remove columns from the final/target dataset. Select the required columns and click on **Continue**.
11. Click on **Save** and then **Save Recipe**.

 We can create an efficient recipe by understanding target dataset requirements.

Running a recipe

Einstein provides the flexibility to only save the recipe if we do not want to create a target dataset. Einstein provides two options, **Save Recipe** and **Save As New…**. Use **Save Recipe** to only save the recipe and use **Save As New…** to create a different transformation without changing the original recipe, as shown in the following screenshot:

 When you use **Save as New…**, change the name of the recipe or run only one recipe to avoid the creation of a dataset of the same name.

To create a target dataset, the user should run the recipe. The user can either run the new recipe to create a new target dataset or use an existing one. To create a target dataset, perform the following steps:

1. Click on the **Create Dataset** button on the recipe page

2. You should see a **RUN RECIPE** dialog box, as shown in the following screenshot:

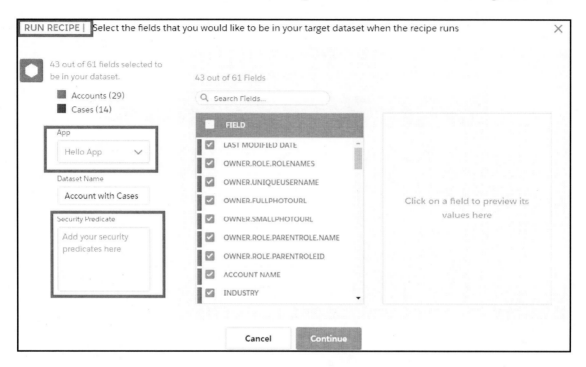

3. You can change the **App** location to save the target dataset
4. Add **Security Predicate** if required
5. Click on **Continue**
6. The user can either opt to run the recipe only once or schedule it to run periodically, as shown in the following screenshot:

Adding data

Use the **Add Data** button to add new data from other datasets to the recipe. When we add new data to the recipe, we need to select a common value field as a merge key field. For example, when we combine data from **Account** and **Opportunity**, we have the ID from the **Account** object and `AccountId` from the opportunity object. Click on the **Add Data** button to add data from a different dataset.

The column profile option

The column profile gives a lot of information about data, such as data insights, the quality of the data, the frequency of values, valid values, null values, and so on. It also gives suggestions on transformations so that the user can build a clean dataset and reduce/remove the inconsistency. To check the column profile to review data insights and quality, take a look at the following steps:

1. Open your recipe and select a column whose column profile needs to be reviewed, as shown in the following screenshot:

The highlighted button will display the column profile

2. Click on the 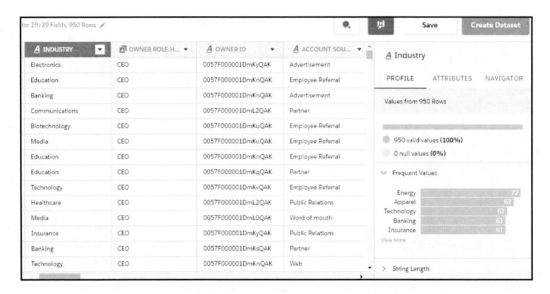 button. It should open the column profile on the right, as shown in the following screenshot:

The user can see three tabs in the column profile, **PROFILE**, **ATTRIBUTES**, and **NAVIGATOR,** as shown in the following screenshot:

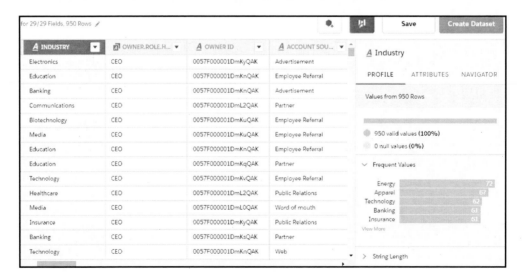

The ATTRIBUTES tab

The **ATTRIBUTES** tab gives information about the field/column selected. It gives information such as **API Name**, **Field Label**, and **Field Type** (whether the selected field is **Measure** or **Dimension**), as shown in the following screenshot:

The NAVIGATOR tab

Depending upon the number of fields in the transformation, the size of the preview increases. The more fields, the larger the data recipe preview and it becomes difficult to get to the required fields. The navigator simplifies things in this scenario. Use the navigator to quickly find the required field and switch between fields, as shown in the following screenshot:

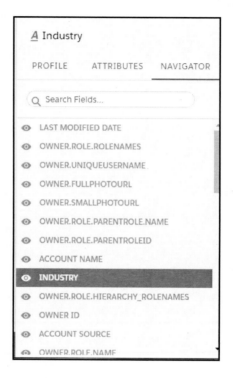

You can use the field navigator to search for required fields and hide unnecessary fields.

Additional transformation suggestions

Einstein Analytics knows that combining data from multiple resources or from multiple datasets can cause inconsistency in the data. In the data recipe, a user can do the transformation to such a data to get consistent data in a new target dataset. In the recipe, the user can see transformation suggestions given by Einstein Analytics, such as **Uppercase**, **Lowercase**, and **Substring**, as shown in the following screenshot:

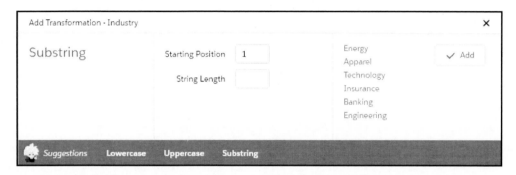

The bucket field

The bucket field gives the user the flexibility to create a new field from the existing values. There is no need to use formula fields. Let's create a bucket field for the **ANNUAL REVENUE** or amount field and categorize it into low, medium, and high values. To add a new bucket field, perform the following steps:

1. Open your saved dataset, `Account with cases`

2. Click on the  icon on the column, as shown in the following screenshot:

3. Click on the **Bucket** field and you should see a panel appear at the bottom, as shown in the following screenshot:

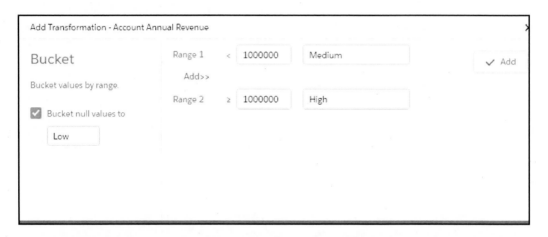

4. Categorize **Bucket null values to** as Low; for **Range 1**, value ranges below **1000000** as Medium, and above as High
5. Click on the **Add** button
6. After clicking on the **Add** button, a new column is added to the recipe for the bucket field

The user can create bucket fields on both **Measures** as well as **Dimensions**. Bucket field values are case-sensitive.

The formula field

The formula field is used to create a field from the existing fields via calculations. You can use all the measures to calculate a new value. In Einstein Analytics, the user can use math functions, arithmetic operators, and so on in the formula field. In the Account with Cases recipe, we have an ANNUAL REVENUE column. Let's create a formula field to get the monthly revenue based on the ANNUAL REVENUE field. To create a formula field, perform the following steps:

1. Open the Account with Cases recipe
2. Search for the column named ANNUAL REVENUE and click on the ⯆ icon in the column

3. Select **Formula** and you should see a formula builder panel appear at the bottom, as shown in the following screenshot:

4. Start typing the field name and the formula builder will suggest related fields, as shown in the following screenshot:

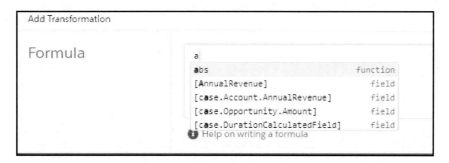

5. Add the [ANNUAL REVENUE]/12 formula and click on the **Add** button
6. Observe that a new Formula column is added to the recipe
7. Save the recipe

The user can also add bucket fields in the formula.

The scheduling recipe

When the user runs a recipe, it applies to all the transformations in the recipe and creates a new target dataset. Einstein Analytics allows the user to schedule a recipe to run on a recurring basis to keep the target dataset up-to-date. To schedule a recipe, perform the following steps:

1. Click on the recipe
2. Click on the **Create Dataset** button on the recipe page and you should see the **Run Recipe** dialog box
3. Click on **Continue**
4. Select the **Yes** radio button and click on **Schedule Recipe**
5. Select the required time, day, and date as shown in the following screenshot:

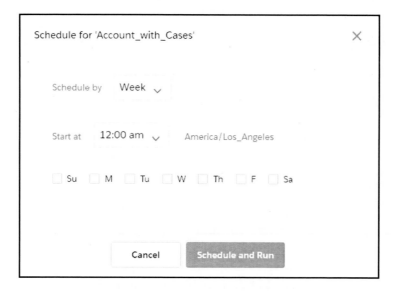

6. Click on **Schedule and Run**

Exporting datasets using datasetUtils

Once the dataflow is complete, it pulls data from the sources and syncs it as a dataset. The dataset stores the data in a format from which Analytics can build visualizations. Using Salesforce Analytics Cloud datasetUtils, the user can now export the dataset. `datasetUtils` are community-developed tools that communicate with Einstein Analytics datasets through an API. The user can also query content using `datasetUtils`. To export data using this tool, perform the following steps:

1. Go to `https://github.com/forcedotcom/Analytics-Cloud-Dataset-Utils/ releases` and download the `datasetUtils.jar` file

2. Run the JAR file and it will open a login window, as shown in the following screenshot:

3. Enter credentials or use **OAuth** to log in
4. Select the dataset
5. Click on the action drop-down menu in the upper-right corner of the screen

6. Choose **Export to CSV**:

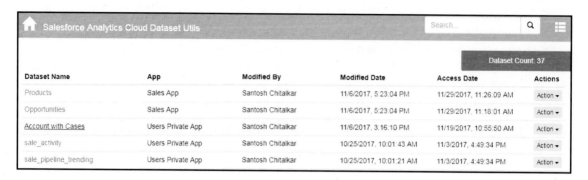

Dataset Name	App	Modified By	Modified Date	Access Date	Actions
Products	Sales App	Santosh Chitalkar	11/6/2017, 5:23:04 PM	11/29/2017, 11:26:09 AM	Action ▾
Opportunities	Sales App	Santosh Chitalkar	11/6/2017, 5:23:04 PM	11/29/2017, 11:18:01 AM	Action ▾
Account with Cases	Users Private App	Santosh Chitalkar	11/6/2017, 3:16:10 PM	11/19/2017, 10:55:50 AM	Action ▾
sale_activity	Users Private App	Santosh Chitalkar	10/25/2017, 10:01:43 AM	11/3/2017, 4:49:34 PM	Action ▾
sale_pipeline_trending	Users Private App	Santosh Chitalkar	10/25/2017, 10:01:21 AM	11/3/2017, 4:49:34 PM	Action ▾

The `datasetUtils` tool does not support derived dimensions and measures. To export a dataset, the user should remove all the derived measures and derived dimensions first. The `datasetUtils` tool is free to use, but it is not officially supported by Salesforce.

Apart from exporting content from Einstein Analytics, the user can also perform the following steps:

1. Download the metadata JSON
2. Edit the XMD file
3. Delete the dataset
4. Search the dataset
5. Edit SAQL
6. Check a list of datasets
7. Check a list of dataflows

Summary

The dataset recipe makes the process of data preparation simpler and we now know how. In this chapter, we learned that the data recipe is a user interface tool that allows you to receive data from existing datasets, replications, bucket fields, and so on, and prepare a new dataset from it. We can export data from Einstein by using `dataset.Utils` but it doesn't support derived measures and derived dimensions. Also, we can create, transform, run, and schedule recipes using **Data Manager**. We can hide and show columns using the navigator.

All datasets and data preparation should be supported by strong security; otherwise, all confidential data will be compromised and may have an effect on the business. Hence, the next chapter is all about security in Einstein Analytics and we are going to study methods to access and restrict Salesforce and dataset records. We are going to explore the configuring integration/security user and sharing applications, lenses, and dashboards.

9
Embedding Einstein Dashboards

Security and sharing in Einstein, which we studied in the previous chapter, gives us the flexibility to share visualizations/dashboards/applications with other users. It's a great and powerful feature. Einstein Analytics knows that a business does not run on a single platform, it runs on multiple platforms, such as Salesforce Classic, Salesforce1, Lightning, or website. Einstein gives users the flexibility to share all powerful visualizations in all Salesforce experiences. This can be done by embedding your dashboards. You can integrate your dashboards in Custom pages, Community sites, Classic, Lightning, and so on. In this chapter, we are going to cover the following topics:

- Embedding dashboards on the detail page in Salesforce Classic
- Embedding dashboards in Lightning
- Viewing Analytics on Communities or Enable Analytics for Communities
- Whitelisting trusted websites for embedded dashboards
- Embedding dashboards on the record page and filtering them depending upon records in Classic and Lightning
- Limitations of embedded Analytics dashboards

Embedding dashboards

The user can embed an Einstein dashboard into a Salesforce record or object. After embedding dashboards, all the metrics, KPIs, and trends can be pulled from the record. Embedding the dashboard with records gives you an interactive presentation. The following diagram explains how, when, and where we can embed dashboards:

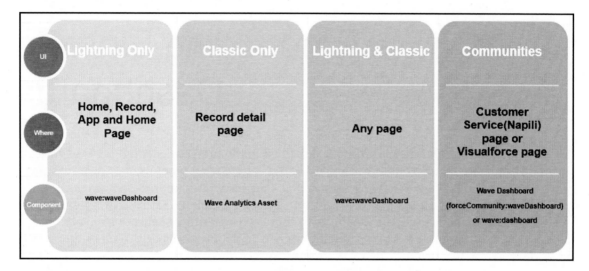

We have to enable View Analytics in Communities Pages Permissions, so that the external users can view dashboards embedded in Visualforce Pages for their communities. Once you enable the Communities Permission Set license, it automatically enables View Analytics on Communities Pages Permission.

Embedding dashboards on the detail page in Salesforce Classic

In order to start embedding the dashboard, let's create a sample dashboard by performing the following steps:

1. Navigate to **Analytics Studio** I **Create** I **Dashboard.**

2. Add three chart widgets on the dashboard.

3. Click on the ⟪ Chart ⟫ button in the middle and select the **Opportunity** dataset. Select **Measures** as **Sum of Amount** and select **BillingCountry** under **Group by**. Click on **Done**.

4. Repeat the second step for the second widget, but select **Account Source** under **Group by** and make it a donut chart.

5. Repeat the second step for the third widget but select **Stage** under **Group by** and make it a funnel chart.

6. Click on Save (s) and enter `Embedding Opportunities` in the title field, as shown in the following screenshot:

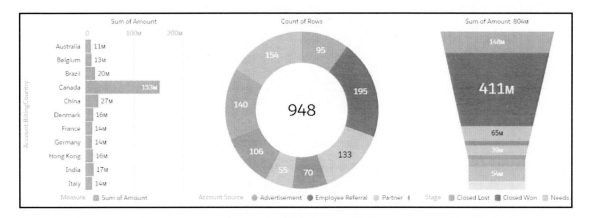

The preceding screenshot displays the data from Opportunities

Now that we have created a dashboard, let's embed this dashboard in Salesforce Classic. In order to start embedding the dashboard, exit from the Einstein Analytics platform and go to Classic mode. The user can embed the dashboard on the record detail page layout in Salesforce Classic. The user can view the dashboard, drill in, and apply a filter, just like in the Einstein Analytics window. Let's add the dashboard to the account detail page by performing the following steps:

1. Navigate to **Setup** | **Customize** | **Accounts** | **Page Layouts** as shown in the following screenshot:

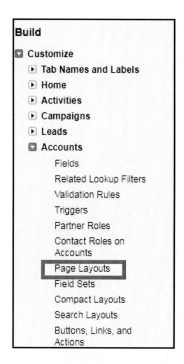

2. Click on **Edit** of **Account Layout** and it will open a page layout editor which has two parts: a palette on the upper portion of the screen, and the page layout on the lower portion of the screen. The palette contains the user interface elements that you can add to your page layout, such as **Fields**, **Buttons, Links, and Actions**, and **Related Lists**, as shown in the following screenshot:

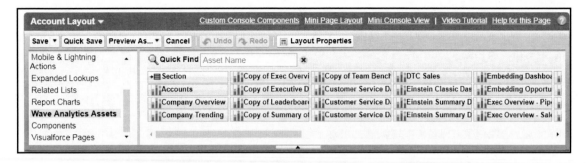

3. Click on the **Wave Analytics Assets** option from the palette and you can see all the dashboards on the right-side panel.

4. Drag and drop a section onto the page layout, name it `Einstein Dashboard`, and click on **OK**.

5. Drag and drop the dashboard which you wish to add to the record detail page. We are going to add `Embedded Opportunities`.

6. Click on **Save**. Go to any accounting record and you should see a new section within the dashboard:

Users can easily configure the embedded dashboards by using attributes. To access the dashboard properties, go to edit page layout again, and go to the section where we added the dashboard to the layout. Hover over the dashboard and click on the ⚒ icon. It will open an **Asset Properties** window:

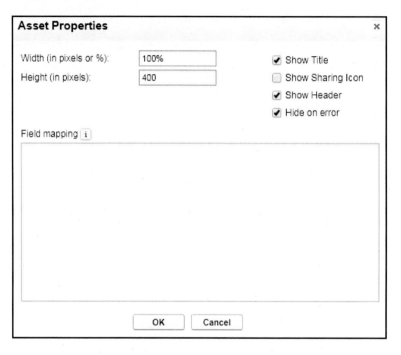

The **Asset Properties** window gives the user the option to change the following features:

- **Width (in pixels or %)**: This feature allows you to adjust the width of the dashboard section.
- **Height (in pixels)**: This feature allows you to adjust the height of the dashboard section.
- **Show Title**: This feature allows you to display or hide the title of the dashboard.
- **Show Sharing Icon**: Using this feature, by default, the share icon is disabled. The **Show Sharing Icon** option gives the user a flexibility to include the share icon on the dashboard.

- **Show Header**: This feature allows you to display or hide the header.
- **Hide on error**: This feature gives you control over whether the Analytics asset appears if there is an error.
- **Field mapping**: Last but not least, field mapping is used to filter the relevant data to the record on the dashboard. To set up the dashboard to show only the data that's relevant to the record being viewed, use field mapping. Field mapping links data fields in the dashboard to the object's fields. We are using the `Embedded Opportunity` dashboard. Let's add field mapping to it. The following is the format for field mapping:

```
{
        "datasets": {
                "datasetName":[{
                        "fields":["Actual Field name from object"],
                        "filter":{"operator": "matches",
"values":["$dataset
                        fieldname"]}
                        }]
        }
```

Let's add field mapping for `account` by using the following format:

```
{
        "datasets": {
                "account":[{
                        "fields":["Name"],
                        "filter":{"operator": "matches",
"values":["$Name"]}
                        }]
                }
        }
```

If your dashboard uses multiple datasets, then you can use the following format:

```
{
        "datasets": {
                "datasetName1":[{
                        "fields":["Actual Field name from object"],
                        "filter":{"operator": "matches",
"values":["$dataset1
                        fieldname"]}
                        }],
                "datasetName2":[{
                        "fields":["Actual Field name from object"],
                        "filter":{"operator": "matches",
"values":["$dataset2
```

```
                              fieldname"]}
                        }]
            }
```

Let's add field mapping for `account` and `opportunities`:

```
{
        "datasets": {
            "opportunities":[{
                            "fields":["Account.Name"],
                            "filter":{"operator":
"matches",
                            "values":["$Name"]}
                        }],
            "account":[{
                            "fields":["Name"],
                            "filter":{"operator": "matches",
                            "values":["$Name"]}
                        }]
        }
    }
```

Now that we have added field mapping, save the page layout and go to the actual record. Observe that the dashboard is getting filtered now per record, as shown in the following screenshot:

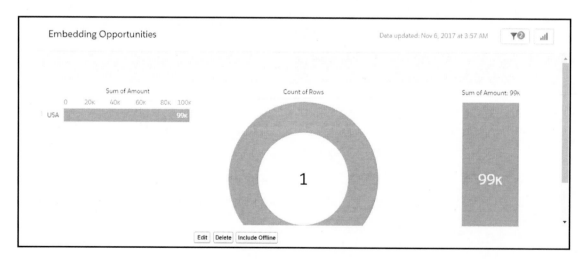

Embedding the dashboard in Lightning

We can add an Einstein Analytics dashboard to three different locations in Lightning, such as **Home Page**, **Record Page**, and **App Page**. The dashboards added to Lightning are flexible enough to drill down and explore the same page.

To add the dashboard to Lightning pages, perform the following steps:

1. Open your org in Lightning Experience.
2. Click on **Setup** and click on **Lightning App Builder** under **User Interface**.
3. Click on **New** and you will be directed to the following page:

4. Select **Record Page** and click on **Next**.

5. Enter the label name under **Label** and select the **Object** where you want to embed the dashboard, as shown in the following screenshot:

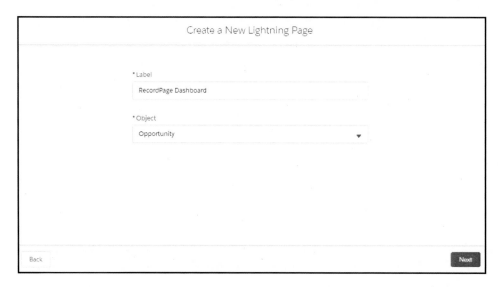

6. Click on **Next** and select the page template on the next screen. We are going to select **Header and One Column**, as shown in the following screenshot:

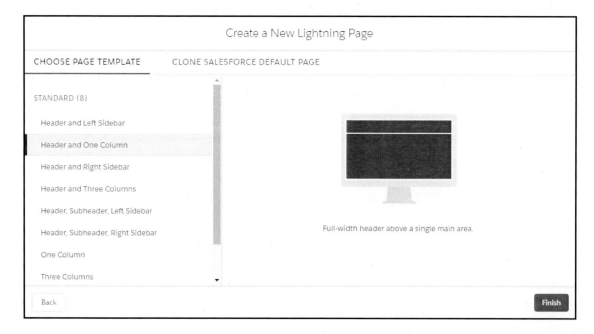

7. Click on **Finish** and you should see the Lightning page created.
8. Search for **Wave Dashboard** in the component list and select it:

The preceding screenshot shows the dashboard displayed after selecting Lightening App Builder

Lightning page attributes in embedding a dashboard

Einstein Analytics provides the user with the attributes through which the user can easily configure the embedded dashboards. Attributes, such as **Show Header** and **Show Title**, give the user the flexibility to quickly change the visibility. The following are some other attributes that are very useful and easy to implement:

- Using the **Open Links in New Windows** attribute, the user can decide where the link from the dashboard should open:

- The user can also adjust the height of the template using the **Height** attribute.
- By default, the sharing icon is hidden. The **Show Sharing Icon** option gives the user the flexibility to include the share icon on the dashboard. The user can use this option to share the image of the dashboard. Post it to Chatter after enabling this option.
- The filter option can be used to add the dynamic filter to the dashboard. When we embed the dashboard to the record page, we can filter the dashboard and update it per record. Use the given code snippet to filter the dashboard:

```
{'datasets':
    {'opportunities':
        [{
            'fields':['Account.Name'],
            'filter':{'operator': 'matches',
'values':['$Name']}
        }]
    }
}
```

After adding all the desired configurations, click on the **Save** button and then the **Activation...** button to activate the embedded dashboard:

The preceding screenshot displays the dashboard after adding the Account Id filter

Embedding the dashboard in Visualforce Pages

We can embed the Analytics dashboard on a Visualforce page just like we embed it on the record detail page for Salesforce Classic. In order to embed the dashboard in a Visualforce page, we have to use the `<wave:dashboard>` component. The user can configure the dashboard using attributes of the component, such as `dashboardId`, `filter`, `showTitle`, and so on. Before starting to embed the dashboard to a Visualforce page, we need to get the dashboard ID. To get the dashboard ID, perform the following steps:

1. Switch to Analytics mode again.
2. Navigate to **Analytics Studio** | **DASHBOARDS** and open the dashboard which you want to embed. We are going to use `Emedded Opportunities`.
3. Check the URL shown in the following screenshot:

4. Copy the dashboard ID that starts with **0F.**

Now that we have the dashboard ID that we want to embed, let's create a new Visualforce page for it. To embed a dashboard in Visualforce Pages, perform the following steps:

1. Exit from Analytics and switch to Classic mode (if you are in Lightning Experience):

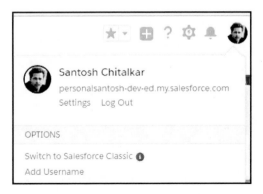

2. Go to **Setup** | **Develop** | **Visualforce Pages** or simply type `visualforce pages` in the **Quick Find / Search...** box:

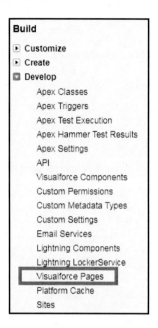

3. Click on **Visualforce Pages** and hit the **New** button to create a new Visualforce page
4. Enter the Visualforce page label `embedded_dashboard` and add the following code:

```
<apex:page standardController="Account">
    <wave:dashboard dashboardId="0FK7F000000HK5WWAW"
    showTitle="true"
    height="800px"
    openLinksInNewWindow="true"/>
</apex:page>
```

5. Replace your dashboard ID in the `dashboardId` attribute
6. Click on **Save** and hit the **Preview** button

Your dashboard is now embedded in the Visualforce page and it is completely interactive.

You can add only one dashboard to a Visualforce page. Users can drill in and explore the dashboard within the frame on the Visualforce page or in a new window in Analytics.

Embedding dashboards to websites and web applications

The user can also embed the Analytics dashboard to websites or any web-based application. In order to do so, we first need to whitelist the website or web application in the Analytics whitelist. Whitelisting a website is nothing other than declaring a website as a trusted site and granting safe access to dashboards. Once the website is whitelisted, the user can access Analytics dashboards in websites and applications outside of Salesforce servers. To whitelist a website, perform the following steps:

1. Switch to Classic mode
2. From **Setup**, enter `Whitelist` in the **Quick Find / Search...** box
3. Select **Whitelist** under **Analytics**, as shown in the following screenshot:

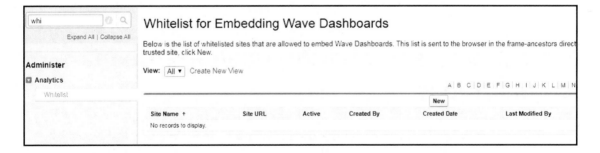

4. Click on **New** and enter your trusted website name and URL, as shown in the following screenshot:

5. Click on **Save**

By default, Salesforce.com and force.com are whitelisted.

Embedding and sharing dashboards in communities

The user can also share the Einstein Analytics dashboard with communities. External users can view applications that are shared with them. The user can embed the dashboard by using either Community Builder or Visualforce Pages. In order to use this feature, users should have Customer Community Plus or a Partner Community license. We can embed Analytics dashboards by using the following steps:

1. Enabling Communities
2. Enabling Analytics for Communities
3. Embedding dashboards using Community Builder or Visualforce
4. Enabling sharing with Communities
5. Inviting Community partners and customers to share the application

Enabling Communities

Communities are the best way for customers and partners to collaborate. Users can create and configure public as well as private communities, which can allow members of the same community to connect directly. To enable Communities, perform the following steps:

1. Switch to Classic mode
2. Go to **Setup** and search for **Communities** in the **Quick Find / Search...** box
3. Click on **Communities Settings** and select the checkbox **Enable communities** as shown in the following screenshot:

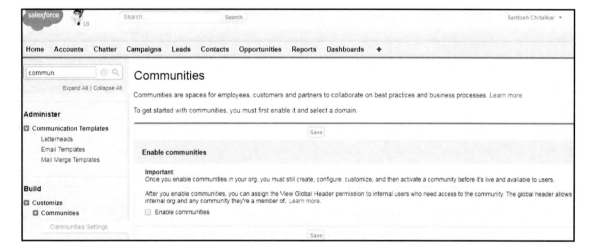

4. Enter the domain name and check the availability
5. Click on **Save**

After enabling Communities, we have to create, configure, customize, and then activate a community. Let's create a new community by executing the following steps:

1. Switch to Classic mode.
2. Go to **Setup** and search for **Communities** in the **Quick Find / Search...** box.

3. Click on **All Communities**, as shown in the following screenshot:

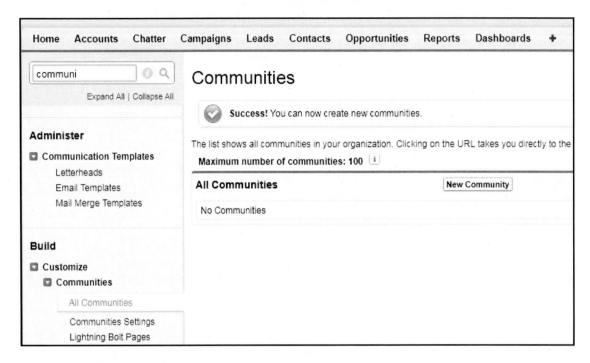

4. Click on **New Community**.
5. Click on **Customer Service (Napili)** and click on the **Get Started** button on the next screen.
6. Enter the name of the community and click on the **Create** button, as shown in the following screenshot:

7. Your community is created. Now, exit from the community.

Enabling Analytics for Communities

In order to share the Analytics dashboard with a Community user, the first step is to enable it for Communities. To use this feature, the user must have Customer Community Plus or a Partner Community license. To enable Analytics for Communities, perform the following steps:

1. Switch to Classic mode (if you are not already in it)
2. Go to **Setup** and search for **Analytics** from the **Quick Find / Search...** box

3. Select **Settings** under **Analytics**, as shown in the following screenshot:

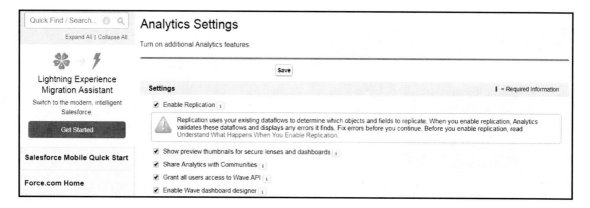

4. Select/check the checkbox **Share Analytics with Communities**
5. Click on **Save**

 The user can embed the Analytics dashboard in Communities, but not in portals.

Embedding dashboards using Community Builder or Visualforce Pages

Community Builder is a very simple point and click functionality provided by Salesforce and is used to create custom communities. Community Builder is available in both Salesforce Classic as well as Lightning Experience. Go to Salesforce Classic, and use the following steps to access Community Builder:

1. In the **Quick Find / Search...** box, type `communities` and select **All Communities** as shown in the following screenshot:

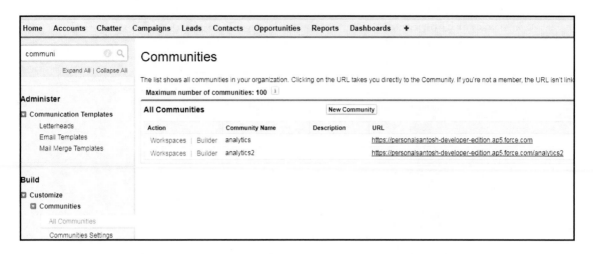

2. Click on **Builder** in your workspace after the community is created. This will open a Community Builder as shown in the following screenshot:

3. Click on **Components** and then select **Wave Dashboard** as shown in the following screenshot:

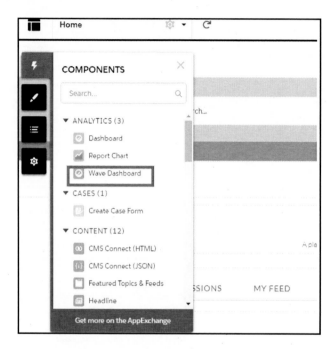

 The user can create up to 100 communities, including all active and inactive communities.

The Enable sharing with Communities option

Now that we can enable sharing Analytics for Communities, we can go ahead and share dashboards with Communities. In order to share dashboards with Communities, you first need to share the entire application with community, and then invite users to access a specific dashboard by performing the following steps:

1. Switch to the Einstein Analytics platform, and click on the ▾ icon of the application in which the desired dashboard is saved, as shown in the following screenshot:

2. Click on **Share**

3. Select the checkbox for **Enable sharing with Communities** on the next screen, as shown in the following screenshot:

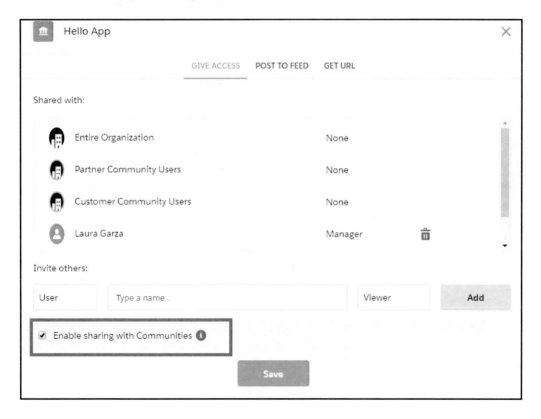

4. Type the name of the community members with whom you wish to share the application/dashboard
5. Click on **Add**
6. Click on **Save**

Summary

Einstein Analytics understands that a business runs on different platforms. Users can embed the dashboards and lenses created in Salesforce Classic, Lightning Experience, Salesforce1, and also in Community. Users do not require any coding for this. Dashboards can be embedded in Lightning Experience by using Lightning App Builder. It is an easy and simple way to embed a dashboard in Lightning Experience. Users can also add dynamic filters to an embedded dashboard by using the filter option with desired configurations. The share icon on the embedded dashboard gives users the flexibility to share the dashboard image with other users in the organization. Embedded dashboards offer **Post to Feed** and **Download sharing** options. The only component used for embedding dashboard in Lightning is `wave:waveDashboard`, and for Classic mode it is **Wave Analytics Asset** from the page layout. Embedded Analytics dashboards can include such features as annotations, notifications, full screen presentation, record actions menus, global filters, links to other Analytics dashboards, and so on.

The next chapter is related to machine-learning and natural-language processing and will provide an overview of two technologies and their uses in Einstein Analytics.

10
Advanced Technologies in Einstein Analytics

There are numerous advanced technologies beyond the basics and no code functionalities, which we discussed. In the previous chapters, we learned about building dashboards, creating lenses, datasets, recipes, and so on. All these features and functionalities help us to create interactive visualizations and give us insight into customer data. Visualizations and insight help businesses make decisions that result in more business and greater customer satisfaction. This chapter will review the advanced and popular technologies in Einstein Analytics. All these technologies help us to create and solve complex business problems that cannot be solved using the basics or the no code approach. Some of these technologies are being used behind the scenes already. For example, Einstein Analytics uses SAQL in lenses and dashboards. The following are the few topics we are going to cover in this chapter:

- Salesforce Analytics Query Language
- XMD
- JSON

Salesforce Analytics Query Language

Just like all other query languages, SAQL retrieves data from the dataset. Lenses and dashboards also use SAQL behind the scenes. It gathers the meaningful data for visualizations.

Using SAQL

There are the following three ways to use SAQL in Einstein Analytics:

- **Creating steps/lenses**: We can use SAQL while creating a lens or step. It is the easiest way of using SAQL. While creating a step, Einstein Analytics provides the flexibility of switching between modes such as Chart Mode, Table Mode, and SAQL Mode. In this chapter, we will use this method for SAQL.
- **Analytics REST API**: Using this API, the user can access the datasets, lenses, dashboards, and so on. This is a programmatic approach and you can send the queries to the Einstein Analytics platform. Einstein Analytics uses the OAuth 2.0 protocol to securely access the platform data. The OAuth protocol is a way of securely authenticating the user without asking them for credentials. The first step to using the Analytics REST API to access Analytics is to authenticate the user using OAuth 2.0.
- **Using Dashboard JSON**: We can use SAQL while editing the Dashboard JSON. We have already seen the Dashboard JSON in previous chapters. To access Dashboard JSON, you can open the dashboard in the edit mode and press *Ctrl + E*.

The simplest way of using SAQL is while creating a step or lens. A user can switch between the modes here. To use SAQL for lens, perform the following steps:

1. Navigate to **Analytics Studio | DATASETS** and select any dataset. We are going to select **Opportunity** here.
2. Click on it and it will open a window to create a lens.
3. Switch to SAQL Mode by clicking on the ⊱ icon in the top-right corner, as shown in the following screenshot:

In SAQL, the query is made up of multiple statements. In the first statement, the query loads the input data from the dataset, operates on it, and then finally gives the result. The user can use the **Run Query** button to see the results and errors after changing or adding statements. The user can see the errors at the bottom of the **Query** editor.

SAQL is made up of statements that take the input dataset, and we build our logic on that. We can add filters, groups, orders, and so on, to this dataset to get the desired output. There are certain order rules that need to be followed while creating these statements and those rules are as follows:

- There can be only one `offset` in the `foreach` statement
- The `limit` statement must be after `offset`
- The `offset` statement must be after `filter` and `order`
- The `order` and `filter` statements can be swapped as there is no rule for them

In SAQL, we can perform all the mathematical calculations and comparisons. SAQL also supports arithmetic operators, comparison operators, string operators, and logical operators.

To add comments in SAQL, you need to add two sequential hyphens, --, at the beginning of the statement. You can add single line comments by using two sequential hyphens.

Using foreach in SAQL

The `foreach` statement applies the set of expressions to every row, which is called **projection**. The `foreach` statement is mandatory to get the output of the query. The following is the syntax for the `foreach` statement:

```
q = foreach q generate expression as 'expresion name';
```

Let's look at one example of using the `foreach` statement:

1. Go to **Analytics Studio | DATASETS** and select any dataset. We are going to select **Opportunity** here.
2. Click on it and it will open a window to create a lens.

3. Switch to SAQL Mode by clicking on the ⟩_ icon in the top-right corner.

   In the **Query** editor you will see the following code:

   ```
   q = load "opportunity";
   q = group q by all;
   q = foreach q generate count() as 'count';
   q = limit q 2000;
   ```

   You can see the result of this query just below the **Query** editor:

```
Query

1   q = load "opportunity";
2   q = group q by all;
3   q = foreach q generate count() as 'count';
4   q = limit q 2000;




Count of Rows

       706
```

4. Now replace the third statement with the following statement:

```
q = foreach q generate sum('Amount') as 'Sum Amount';
```

5. Click on the **Run Query** button and observe the result as shown in the following screenshot:

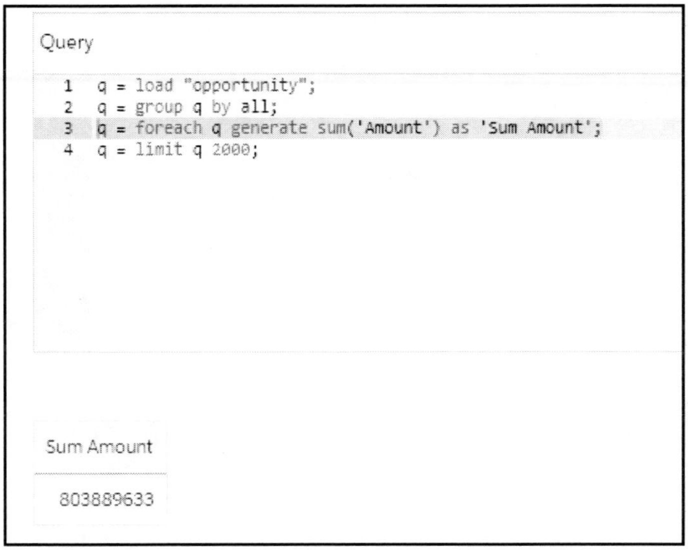

```
Query

1   q = load "opportunity";
2   q = group q by all;
3   q = foreach q generate sum('Amount') as 'Sum Amount';
4   q = limit q 2000;




Sum Amount

803889633
```

Using grouping in SAQL

The user can group records of the same value in one group by using the group statements. Use the following syntax:

```
q = group rows by fieldName
```

Let's see how to use grouping in SAQL by performing the following steps:

1. Replace the second and third statement with the following statement:

```
q = group q by 'StageName';
q = foreach q generate 'StageName' as 'StageName',
sum('Amount') as 'Sum Amount';
```

2. Click on the **Run Query** button and you should see the following result:

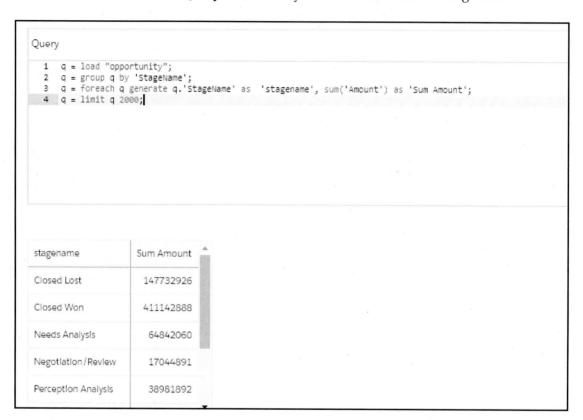

The `cogroup` statement behaves the same as the `group` statement and they are interchangeable.

Using filters in SAQL

Filters in SAQL behave just like a `where` clause in SOQL and SQL, filtering the data as per the condition or clause. In Einstein Analytics, it selects the row from the dataset that satisfies the condition added.

The syntax for the filter is as follows:

```
q = filter q by fieldName 'Operator' value
```

Let's filter the opportunities that are greater than 5.4 million by performing the following steps:

1. Add the following statement just after the dataset is loaded:

```
q = filter q by 'Amount' > 5400000;
```

2. Click on **Run Query** and view the result as shown in the following screenshot:

Query

```
1  q = load "opportunity";
2  q = filter q by 'Amount' > 5400000;
3  q = group q by 'StageName';
4  q = foreach q generate 'StageName' as 'StageName', sum('Amount') as 'Sum Amount';
5  q = limit q 2000;
```

Stage	Sum Amount
Closed Lost	5423800
Closed Won	7747190
Perception Analysis	14417105

Using functions in SAQL

The beauty of a function is in its reusability. Once the function is created it can be used multiple times. In SAQL, we can use different types of functions, such as string functions, math functions, aggregate functions, windowing functions, and so on. These functions are predefined and saved quite a few times. Let's use a math function power.

The syntax for the power is `power(m, n)`. The function returns the value of `m` raised to the nth power. Replace the following statement with the fourth statement:

```
q = foreach q generate 'StageName' as 'StageName',
power(sum('Amount'), 1/2) as 'Amount Squareroot',
sum('Amount') as 'Sum Amount';
```

Click on the **Run Query** button. You can use other functions similarly as well.

SAQL is highly influenced by **Pig-Latin** (**pigql**), a high-level platform for creating programs that run on Apache Hadoop.

Extended metadata in Analytics

In this section, we are going to provide an overview of the extended metadata, and we will go through the basic structure of XMD, how to configure it, and what we can achieve with XMD. The extended metadata or XMD in Einstein Analytics gives the user the flexibility to format and customize the fields and values in the dataset. We are going to use the `Embedded dashboard` and the **Opportunity** dataset from the previous chapter for this.

Downloading the XMD for the dataset

In order to configure the XMD file, first we need to get the XMD file for the dataset. So the question is: where can you find it?

To download the XMD file, perform the following steps:

1. Go to the **Analytics Studio** | **DATASETS** tab.
2. Click on the ⏷ icon in the dataset (we are using the **Opportunity** dataset) and click on **Edit** as shown in the following screenshot:

3. Search for the **Extended Metadata File** section and click on ⬛. You should see two options in the dropdown, such as **Download** and **Replace**, as shown in the following screenshot:

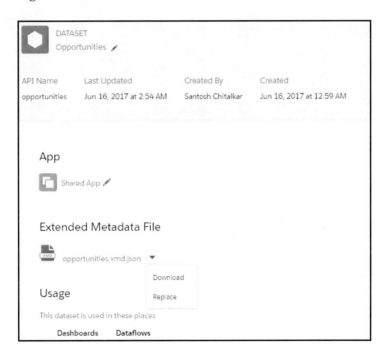

4. Click on **Download** and open the file in the JSON editor or Notepad++.

The XMD file is JSON in such a format that we need to use the JSON editor so that we can see all the parameters and nodes; this makes it easy to make changes to a particular field.

> Make sure that you keep a backup of the original XMD file before editing it. If something goes wrong, you will always have the working copy of XMD.

Configuring XMD

Now that we have the XMD file, we can configure it as per our needs. Open the `Embedded dashboard` dashboard we created in a previous chapter:

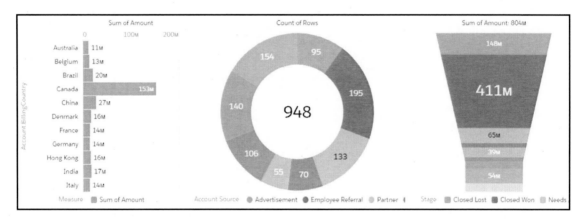

Observe that the **Amount/Currency** field is missing a currency symbol. So let's format the XMD file in such way that it will display the $ symbol for the **Amount** field. In order to achieve this, we need to format the measure. We can apply the symbol before or after the numeric value. To add the $ symbol, perform the following steps:

1. Edit the XMD file we downloaded and copy all code from it by using *Ctrl + A*
2. Use any JSON editor or go to `http://jsoneditoronline.org/` and paste the code in the left-side editor:

3. Search for the `measures` node and `Amount` field on the right side

4. Expand the `format` node and add `"[\"$#,###,###.##\",1]"` to the `customFormat` label as shown in the following code snippet:

```
{
    "field": "sum_Amount",
    "format": {
        "customFormat": "[\"$#,###.00\",1]"
    },
    "label": "sum_Amount",
    "showInExplorer": true
}
```

5. Save the document

Uploading XMD in the dataset

Now that we have made our changes in the XMD, it's time to upload it back in Analytics for the dataset so that it will reflect the changes on the dashboard. To upload XMD back to Analytics, perform the following steps:

1. Go to the **Analytics Studio** | **DATASETS** tab
2. Click on the icon in the dataset (we are using the **Opportunity** dataset) and click on **Edit** as shown in the following screenshot:

3. Search for **Extended Metadata File** and click on
4. Select **Replace** and upload the configured file
5. Now open the `Embedded dashboard` dashboard again and observe that the $ symbol is appearing now:

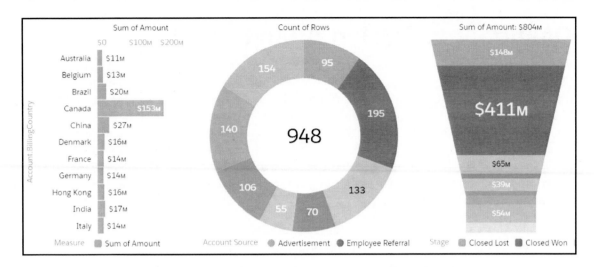

Similarly, we can achieve the preceding configuration by making the following changes in the XMD file:

1. Change display labels for dataset fields
2. Change display labels for dataset values
3. Format the measures
4. Change chart colors for dimension values
5. Add actions to dimensions

 When you modify the XMD file for the dataset, it reflects the changes in all visualizations that use the dataset.

Dashboard JSON in Analytics

We know that we can build lenses and dashboards by using Wave Analytics Dashboard Designer or Classic Designer. It is an easy no code approach that gives us insight into the data. The user can build clean and meaningful dashboards for business using this approach. However, sometimes this is not enough for complex or more customized dashboards. In this case, we need to edit Dashboard JSON. We need to modify the Dashboard JSON file to do advanced customization. We have already gone through a couple of assignments in previous chapters where we have edited Dashboard JSON. Dashboard JSON decides how the components on the dashboards should interact with each other. Using Dashboard JSON, we can perform the following steps:

1. Manual binding of the components and the steps
2. Binding static step to other components on the dashboard
3. Setting the row limits
4. Setting filters
5. Creating dynamic and complex queries
6. Setting the layout
7. Adding the column values
8. We can access the Dashboard JSON by opening a dashboard in edit mode and then pressing *Ctrl + E* on Windows

Summary

The idea of including this chapter was to give you an overview of the three advanced technologies Einstein Analytics has to build complex and customized dashboards and solutions. The user can use SAQL to retrieve data from the dataset and create advanced lenses. While using SAQL, the user can use different functions such as math functions, string functions, arithmetic functions, and so on. The XMD file can be configured to achieve the formatting of the dashboard, fields, and values. In order to change the formatting using XMD, we need to download the file, make the changes, and upload it again. While doing this, make sure that you have a backup of the original XMD.

Last but not least, Dashboard JSON. Dashboard JSON is used to build advanced dashboards. The Dashboard JSON file defines how the components on the dashboard should interact with each other. Using Dashboard JSON, we can bind static steps with other steps, set the limits, build complex queries, and so on.

11

Machine Learning and Deep Learning

In the previous chapter, we learned about embedding the Einstein Analytics dashboards in Lightning, Salesforce Classic, and Community. The power of embedding dashboards into other environments is good for business as it runs on multiple platforms. Until now, we have learned the point and click features, security and sharing, and all the basics that help us to create visualizations that give the business insights and help in making business decisions. Creating lenses, steps, static steps, and charts give key information about the business to the user. All the decisions made the business to grow. We defined the Einstein Analytics as the Analytics powered by AI and, until now, we have not gone through or implemented anything related to AI or how AI works in Einstein Analytics. This chapter is for absolute beginners, we are going to take an overview of AI, Einstein Discovery, deep learning, machine learning, natural-language processing, and predictive analysis in Einstein Analytics.

AI in Einstein Analytics

Artificial Intelligence (AI), also known as machine intelligence, means making a machine think like a human. For example, when a human listens to someone, then the human can interpret their feelings and recognize whether the other person is happy or sad. Humans can understand the sensibility and emotions. When a human sees a picture, they can recognize whether it is flower, car, or building, for example. So making the machine capable enough to think or behave like a human is nothing but AI. In other words, AI is about making programs smarter, to think like humans.

We are already using AI in our day-to-day life. Facebook automatically recognizes the people in the photo you uploaded and suggests names and tags. Facebook also suggests captions for your pictures; this is nothing but AI. Using AI in Salesforce, we can enable the following features:

- Visual detection
- Brand detection
- Image recognition

The core technologies behind the AI in Einstein Analytics are deep learning, machine learning, and natural language-processing. Let's look at each of these concepts.

Machine learning

Machine learning is the core of any AI system. Machine learning is an ability given to a computer to learn from the data without explicitly being programmed. It consumes the data and learns from the data by using complex algorithms.

How is this even possible? How can a machine self-learn from data ?? The answer is "by training data." In a machine learning module, we can train the structured data to use complex algorithms and make predictions on the basis of that.

Deep learning

Now we know that machine learning can be applied to structured data and it will help in the prediction analysis. But the performance of the machine learning degrades a lot when the data is unstructured. Unstructured data also slows down processing in machine learning but important keys can be hidden inside the unstructured data. Deep learning is the best feature to operate on the unstructured data, for example, Google uses the deep learning for facial recognition in photos.

In deep learning, we can train the data using algorithms in such a way that it will recognize the patterns. With this approach, we can get interesting and vital information about the data.

 Deep learning is gaining a lot of popularity because of its method and the insight it gives about the data.

Einstein Vision is one of the Einstein Analytics technologies that harnesses the power of image recognition and uses the deep learning for it. Users can build powerful and fast applications using Einstein Vision without a data scientist. We can use the Einstein Vision's image recognition for the following purposes:

- **Visual search**: Expand the ways that your customers can discover your products and increase sales
- **Brand detection**: Monitor your brand across all your channels to increase your marketing reach and preserve brand integrity
- **Product identification**: Increase the ways that you can identify your products to streamline sales processes and customer service

You can use the following link for more details:

```
https://metamind.readme.io/v1/docs/use-pre-built-models
```

Natural-language processing

Natural-language processing (**NLP**)is the part of the machine learning process where the computer communicates with the human through languages and recognizes the pattern or behavior from the language:

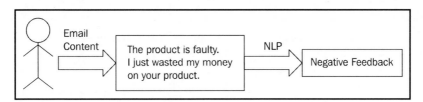

The best application of NLP is the sentiment analysis. In sentiment analysis, the programs recognize the sentiment and emotions of the customer.

Einstein Language is one of the applications that uses the power of NLP to serve the customers in a whole new way. By going through all the unstructured data, Einstein Language gives better insight to the data.

Einstein Intent

Einstein Intent is used to analyze the unstructured customer data and categorize it. This categorized data is then labeled in different classes to understand what exactly the customer is trying to accomplish. The Einstein Intent API creates a module to route the cases to the respective team. The user can analyze the customer text from email, social media such as Facebook and Twitter, and chats and achieve the following:

- Understand what the customer is interested in and the product feature they are looking for
- Provide self-service
- Route the cases to team

Einstein Sentiment

By using NLP, the model of **Einstein Sentiment** can classify the text as positive, negative, or neutral. Einstein Sentiment classifies the sentiment of the customer from the text and analyzes the feelings behind the text. The user can use the Einstein Sentiment API to scan their customers' text from email and social media and analyze the feedback. Using Einstein Sentiment, the user can grow their business and can:

- Know the customer sentiment about their product/service
- Know the current trends
- Provide the customer service first to unsatisfied customer
- Monitor the brand reviews

The current version of Einstein Language only supports the English language.

Summary

Machine learning, deep learning, and NLP are integral parts of the AI. This can help us with making predictions, sentiment analysis, and pattern reorganizations to understand customer needs. Einstein Vision and Einstein Language help the user understand the customer's sentiments and the intent of their text from email, chats, and social media platforms.

We started this book with an introduction to Einstein Analytics and are finishing with machine learning and deep learning. I hope you enjoyed this journey of learning Einstein Analytics. In this book, we learned about basic concepts and terminologies, lenses, and creating dashboards. We explored data recipes, XMD, and embedding into multiple environments. In this chapter, we took an overview of both machine learning and deep learning. The idea of is to combine business intelligence with AI to get data insights and help customers. I wish you luck on your journey to Einstein Analytics and your career.

Other Books You May Enjoy

If you enjoyed this book, you may be interested in these other books by Packt:

Learning Salesforce Einstein
Mohith Shrivastava

ISBN: 978-1-78712-689-3

- Get introduced to AI and its role in CRM and cloud applications
- Understand how Einstein works for the sales, service, marketing, community, and commerce clouds
- Gain a deep understanding of how to use Einstein for the analytics cloud
- Build predictive apps on Heroku using PredictionIO, and work with Einstein Predictive Vision Services
- Incorporate Einstein in the IoT cloud
- Test the accuracy of Einstein through Salesforce reporting and Wave analytics

Salesforce Lightning Reporting and Dashboards
Johan Yu

ISBN: 978-1-78829-738-7

- Navigate in Salesforce.com within the Lightning Experience User Interface
- Secure and share your reports and dashboards with other users
- Create, manage, and maintain reports using Report Builder
- Learn how the report type can affect the report generated
- Explore the report and dashboard folder and the sharing model
- Create reports with multiple formats and custom report types
- Explore various dashboard features in Lightning Experience
- Use Salesforce1, including accessing reports and dashboard

Leave a review - let other readers know what you think

Please share your thoughts on this book with others by leaving a review on the site that you bought it from. If you purchased the book from Amazon, please leave us an honest review on this book's Amazon page. This is vital so that other potential readers can see and use your unbiased opinion to make purchasing decisions, we can understand what our customers think about our products, and our authors can see your feedback on the title that they have worked with Packt to create. It will only take a few minutes of your time, but is valuable to other potential customers, our authors, and Packt. Thank you!

Index